HOW THEY GOT INTO HARVARD

Also by *The Harvard Crimson*

50 Successful Harvard Application Essays

HOW THEY GOT INTO HARVARD

By the Staff of
The Harvard Crimson

 St. Martin's Griffin ✖ NEW YORK

www.stmartins.com

Library of Congress Cataloging-in-Publication Data Available upon Request

ISBN 0-312-34375-2
EAN 978-0-312-34375-0

10   9   8

Contents

Strategy 1: Flaunt Your Talent and Get Recruited

Strategy 2: Be Passionate

Strategy 3: Find the Perfect Balance

Strategy 8: Make Yourself Heard and Campaign to Win

Acknowledgments

First and foremost, we wish to thank our tireless and wonderful editor at St. Martin's, Tom Mercer, for helping us generate the original idea for the book and for constantly motivating us to see this project all the way through. Also, once we had our initial inspiration, our agent, Linda Mead, was extremely helpful as we worked on the official proposal to St. Martin's. We could not have done it without you two.

In addition, we wish to thank the fifty students who were willing to share their stories with us and the world in this book. We loved working with all of you and were truly inspired by each and every one of you.

We also want to extend our gratitude to all of the members of the *Crimson* staff, without whom this book would not have been possible. From interviewing to editing, we appreciate your hard work on this book despite still having to meet your daily deadlines. Keep the old sheet flying!

Finally, we wish to dedicate this book to all the *Crimson* editors who benefit from *The Harvard Crimson*'s financial aid program, now and in the future.

Best of luck in all you do,

Lauren A. E. Schuker ('06), President, *The Harvard Crimson*, 2005–2006
Erica K. Jalli ('05), President, *The Harvard Crimson*, 2004–2005

Introduction

The Harvard College class of 2009 saw a record 22,796 applicants this year, but only 2,074 acceptances were offered, for an admission rate of 9.1 percent. Fifty-six percent of the candidates scored a 1400 or higher on the SATs, while 3,200 were valedictorians of their high school classes. These ultra-talented and highly motivated applicants expressed a wide range of extracurricular interests as well. These days, the college admissions game is a very expensive, high-pressure process. More and more students are working with private SAT tutors and college admissions advisors in high school, and the process can start as early as parents competing to get their children admitted to the "right" preschools.

With such tough competition, we know how hard it is to stand out. We have been through the rigorous selection process ourselves, and have often wished that we knew then what we know now. While *The Harvard Crimson*'s initial book, *50 Successful Harvard Application Essays*, was a successful guide on how to craft an interesting, articulate, and successful college essay, we wanted to take an even more comprehensive look at the application process. Thus, *How They Got into Harvard* was born. By examining the entire application process from start to finish, we wish to give college applicants an edge by distilling the most successful proven admissions tactics in the game. We hope to give students the self-presentation tools to achieve success not only in the admissions process, but throughout their college and post-college careers.

Our Mission

Each day, the editors of *The Harvard Crimson* have the privilege of meeting, interviewing, and working with talented, fascinating, and diverse students in the Harvard community. Through these daily interactions, we have witnessed how each Harvard undergraduate has a unique story behind his or her admission to the college.

How They Got into Harvard is a comprehensive look into the admissions process of an elite college. We have profiled fifty successful applicants who used one of eight key strategies that we have identified to help any student get into the college of his or her choice. In a day and age where it appears that there are standard formulas for admissions success, we aim to show students that applicants who tailored their applications, essays, and college careers to highlight their strengths performed best and turned out the happiest. Our goal is to show how students used tried and true strategies to get themselves noticed and show off their individual talents, thus getting that competitive edge in the application process.

How They Got into Harvard is not meant to serve as a template to be strictly followed, but rather as a resource to guide and inspire originality in your own application. One important thing to note is that the information for each student varies, as the students profiled in this book are from all over the world. For example, secondary school statistics and experiences will vary widely, though we have made our best attempt to standardize this information as much as possible. By reading through each of the different profiles, it becomes clear that while these applicants are all very different in their backgrounds and achievements, they share the fact that they are all aware of what their strengths are. They use this self-knowledge to their advantage not only in the admissions process, but well into their college careers and beyond.

These students packaged themselves in a variety of innovative ways, but they were not afraid to stand out or to simply be themselves. Whether they combined a love for film and field hockey to gain early admission, or leveraged their experiences in the military to transfer into the college of their choice, they all share one thing: a passion that resonates in everything they do and the drive to make things happen. We hope that as you read, you are as inspired by these students as we were when we interviewed them.

How to Use This Book

We have distilled the secrets to gaining admission to elite colleges like Harvard into eight key strategies and provided in-depth profiles of students who used at least one these approaches to successfully gain admission. You can use one of these strategies, or even a few that suit you, depending on your background and circumstances. As you will see from the profiles, the students themselves often used a combination of tactics to achieve victory in the process.

FLAUNT YOUR TALENT AND GET RECRUITED

Are you a champion or protégé who is constantly in the headlines? Then be proud of your skills and display them prominently throughout the admissions process. Everyone you meet and everything you do during the process should emphasize your talent.

BE PASSIONATE

Passion pulls at the heartstrings of admissions officers, so flaunt it! Put your heart and soul into your application and show how your sincerity and passion resonate in everything you do and with everyone you meet!

FIND THE PERFECT BALANCE

These classic, well-rounded students did it all—and they did it well. You may have to wear many hats to pull this off, but it's no "hat trick" if you have what it takes!

LEAD THE PACK

Show the admissions office that you are a visionary, a motivator, a team player, and a trailblazer. Check out how these head honchos got everyone around them to sing their praises!

BEAT THE ODDS

Everyone's situation is different and it's impossible for admissions officers to know what you had to overcome or how hard you had to work to become the person you are unless you tell them! Show the admissions office how you went above and beyond what was asked or expected to thrive in a difficult environment.

WRITE THE STANDOUT ESSAY

If you can make words jump off the page, evoke tears or laughter, or think you are the next Shakespeare, use the essay to your advantage! This is your chance to be as expressive and original as possible—just check out the great examples we have here!

MAKE AND USE CONNECTIONS

Find *your* six degrees of separation. Tapping into the network is initially difficult, but if you keep your eyes and ears open at the start, once you get in you'll find an abundance of admissions resources at your fingertips!

MAKE YOURSELF HEARD AND CAMPAIGN TO WIN

The squeaky wheel gets the grease! It's true even in admissions. There are thousands of other kids applying—read all about how these applicants were rewarded for their persistence.

In order to produce this book, *The Harvard Crimson* editorial staff came together and brainstormed how to structure the information so as to best convey the application process. Once we settled on how we would present the information, we sought to interview the most interesting Harvard students with varied backgrounds, interests, and talents. Each student has a very different recollection of his or her application process, so the profiles vary a bit in voice and amount of information provided. Some students vividly recall desiring to attend Harvard since kindergarten, while others decided to apply completely on a whim. Some students remember exactly what they were thinking while they painstakingly crafted their application, while others were thrust into the process simply because Harvard accepts the common application. Regardless of how well these students remember certain parts of the process relative to others, they shared how they felt about the process overall and what steps they took to ensure their success. For some, the interview was their moment to shine, while others made their passion come through on paper. Each profile reflects an individual personality, voice, and experience, and while you may not be able to personally relate to all fifty featured students, we hope that you are able to find them motivational and helpful in your own college application process.

And good luck.

—*Lauren A. E. Schuker and Erica K. Jalli*

HOW THEY GOT INTO HARVARD

Strategy 1: Flaunt Your Talent and Get Recruited

This chapter is all about playing to your strengths. From athletics to the arts, it is crucial that those who excel in one particular field show how that success has carried over to various other aspects of their lives. The key here is balance. In this chapter, we see students who have developed drive and discipline through their various activities and have channeled that energy from the field and the stage into the classroom as well as into the community. These students got Harvard's attention by making headlines and making solid connections with their future coaches and teammates.

There are various approaches for using your skill or athletic ability to your advantage. A lot of these students showed that they could balance various activities and excel at all of them. For instance, Mary Serdakowski and Gareth James Doran both discussed their abilities to balance sports and academics in their application, and how the discipline they developed through their sport transferred into everything else they did. Another strategy is to include supplementary materials in your application. For instance, Julia Scott Carey included recordings in her application, while Bong Ihn Koh attached a résumé that solely featured his musical achievements to his regular résumé and application. Finally, get recruited! Zak Farkes and Aliaa Remtilla got themselves on the Harvard coaches' radar screens early so that they could meet future teammates and prepare their applications appropriately.

This strategy is not for everyone. It is important that you have a realistic notion of how talented you are in a given field before you choose to make that the focus of your application process. As you'll see here, even national champions made sure they were well balanced in all areas. If you are a state or national champion in your chosen activity, you are a very good candidate for this strategy.

Make sure you speak to your college counselor and other mentors to get an accurate assessment, however, of how much you should focus on your talent. If you choose to pursue this route, you should do the following:

- Include supplementary materials (practice or performance videos, CDs, portfolios, newspaper clippings).
- Contact the coach/team/activity advisor early on and in person, if possible.
- Network with others in your field to get contacts at the college and elsewhere who can help you out.
- Find a mentor to help you through the application process.
- BALANCE! Choose one medium (essay, interview, etc.), to showcase another side of yourself.

Harvard loves students who are extremely talented and will achieve further greatness on campus, so flaunt your talent, but make sure that you show that you can contribute to the college in a variety of other ways as well.

Racquel Bracken

Hometown: Irving, TX (suburban)
High School: Private school, 100 students in graduating class
GPA: 3.8
SAT: 760 Math, 740 Verbal
Extracurriculars: Captain of the debate team, president of the National Honor Society, varsity swimming record holder, community service volunteer at a children's hospital, staff writer of student-run newspaper, volunteer Spanish-language translator.

Summer Activities: Three years of summer debate institute, including one year as Kentucky Fellow at the University of Kentucky debate tournament (taught a group of thirty high school students, participated in mock-debates for exhibition, taught and led research teams). Summer before freshman year, member of Dallas Mustangs national-level swim team. Volunteered at a children's hospital in the children's intensive care unit.

Awards: National Debate Champion and various speech awards (won the Glenbrooks National Tournament in 2000, won the Barkley Forum National Debate Tournament at Emory University in 2001, second at the NFL National Tournament in 2001). School swimming record holder in the 100 butterfly.

Family Background and Education: Her father graduated from the University of Oklahoma–Norman, and was a pilot, small-business owner, and farmer. Her mother graduated from Yonsei University in Seoul, South Korea, where she received her M.D.

Nationality/Ethnicity: Asian-American

College Acceptances: Harvard (early admission)

College Rejections: None

When Racquel Bracken won her first national debate championship in 2000, she could not help but think that the title would be a nice addition to her college application. But the then-teenager from Irving, Texas, knew that getting into Harvard required more than fame. Recognizing that other prospective applicants would have distinguished themselves in a variety of pursuits, Racquel was worried that she had had to give up too much for debate. Her challenge, she thought, was to convince the admissions office that her excellence in debate, however limited, was evidence of her ability to commit wholeheartedly to a single pursuit.

High School

From first grade onward, Racquel attended the Greenhill School in Dallas, a private school with 105 students in the senior class. A serious scholar, Racquel finished high school fifth among her classmates with a 3.8 grade-point average. The president of the National Honor Society, she was also a varsity swimmer and runner, and wrote for her school newspaper. These activities, however, were secondary to the one extracurricular that earned her headlines of her own: debate.

Racquel and her partner were two-time national champions in the cross-examination division. A four-year member of the team, Racquel also served as its captain. Among the topics she debated were U.S. foreign policy toward Russia, particularly the use of tactical nuclear weapons on the borders of non-NATO states. In her senior year, she argued in favor of ways to prevent identity theft on the Internet. A more than twenty-hour-a-week commitment, debate required Racquel to do extensive research on a variety of topics and to work closely with her partner to practice speedspeaking and argumentation skills. She says the experience of intense competition and the opportunity to travel widely were invaluable. "Within my main activity, debate," she recalls, "I learned about leadership, communication, and teamwork while having an amazing time."

The Application and Essay

While debate provided her with a wealth of experience to draw upon in writing her essay, Racquel also sought to convey to the admissions office her commitment to her family. She wrote her supplementary essay about the goals she had achieved through debate; however, she chose to write her primary essay about her father. She first wrote the piece in rhetoric class her senior year and edited it with the help of her English teacher and debate coach. In only a few pages, she described how, once embarrassed by her dad, she soon began to imitate and emulate him. A recurring theme throughout the essay was the silly jokes he told the employees of a local drive-through restaurant. "By the end of the piece," Racquel recalls, "I was the one sitting in the driver's seat imitating him."

Contacts and Connections

Racquel did not know any faculty or administrators when applying to Harvard, but she was placed on a debate watch list by a friend's father.

While she says she is not sure whether that had any effect, she also turned to a friend from debate who was already at Harvard for help. "I visited her at school, attended some classes, slept in her dorm room, and spoke to her about what she liked about going to Harvard," she says. "She not only helped me get a feel for the school but also opened a new avenue of activities for me to join when I came freshman year." Racquel also had two interviews, one on campus and one in Dallas. She says that they were both easygoing conversations. While she did not write her interviewers thank-you notes immediately afterward, she says she did stay in touch and thanked them months later.

At Harvard

Despite her intense commitment to debate in high school, when Racquel arrived at Harvard she decided to shift her focus. While she still helps coach and judge debate tournaments, she no longer competes and uses the time for a variety of different pursuits. Racquel has run a community service program on campus and swims and plays squash recreationally. She also has found a new passion in laboratory science, and spends dozens of hours a week researching stem cells, a topic she once judged on in a debate tournament.

The Bottom Line

Racquel advises prospective applicants not to be afraid of focusing on one talent in their applications. "I think the most important part of my application was not that I pursued many activities in high school, but rather that I narrowed down what I enjoyed, I had to make choices about what activities were important to me, and then I excelled as best I could in the activities that I loved," she says. Racquel believes that colleges often look for maturity and that the best way to demonstrate it is to show one's ability to make sacrifices for something they love.

—*Jessica E. Vascellaro*

Julia Scott Carey

Hometown: Wellesley, MA (suburban)

High School: Small private boarding and day school, 150 students in graduating class

GPA: No GPAs or rankings used by Julia's school

SAT: 800 Math, 730 Verbal

Extracurriculars: President of French club, chorus, orchestra, and chamber music groups; music lessons at the New England Conservatory Preparatory Division; teaching children music on a volunteer basis.

Summer Activities: Julia attended Boston University's Tanglewood Institute for Composition for three years and spent one summer at the Oxbridge Academic Program in Paris. She also participated in the American Psychological Association's pinnacle summit as a representative young person with a very serious interest in music.

Awards (Music): Frances B. Lanier Award, New England Conservatory of Music; the A. Howard Abell Prize, Milton Academy; American Society of Composers, Authors, and Publishers (ASCAP) Foundation Morton Gould Young Composer Award, 1998–2004; National Foundation for the Advancement of the Arts, Honorable Mention; ASCAP Plus Awards 2000–2003; Rivers Music School Twenty-fifth Annual Seminar on Contemporary Music Composition Prize; International Young Composers Competition, senior division, second prize for *Pas de deux*; Davidson Institute for Talent Development Scholarship Award; American Psychological Association Pinnacle Scholar; Harvard Music Association Composition Prize; Greater Twin Cities Youth Symphonies Peer-to-Peer Commissioning Project Award; Milton Young Musicians Festival, Piano Performance, level 8 gold medal.

Awards (Other): The school's Wales Prize for Science and Bisbee Prize for History, National Merit Finalist, Cum Laude Society.

Family Background and Education: Julia is the second generation in her family to go to an Ivy League school. Her mother attended Harvard and her father attended Columbia and Harvard. Julia's mother was an emergency room physician who stopped working when Julia was born, and her father is an investment manager.

Nationality/Ethnicity: Caucasian/Irish-American
College Acceptances: Harvard (early admission)
College Rejections: None

Julia's success in getting accepted to Harvard most likely stems from her incredible musical talents and dedication to this interest. "The most basic thing about me is that I'm a musician and music has always been the most important thing in my life outside of schoolwork," says Julia Scott Carey. As a precocious five-year-old, Julia developed her own system of writing down the notes that made up her pieces; now she is a composer who has had many of her pieces performed by orchestras or ensembles and also plays the piano, harpsichord, and flute, and sings. In high school most of Julia's commitments lay outside of school, but she says she believes that that made her more independent. She credits her early composition opportunities in part to a great community orchestra in her hometown, with an orchestra director who encouraged her.

Julia grew up with her parents and one younger sister in Wellesley, Massachusetts, likes going to Martha's Vineyard and reading Wodehouse novels, and used to ride horses. She enjoys traveling and has been to St. Petersburg, Russia, four times for music competitions and performance. In high school, Julia also had an interest in visual arts and enjoyed painting.

High School

In high school, Julia served as President of the French club, but focused on her involvement with musical groups: the school chorus and orchestra and chamber music groups. Passionate about her music, Julia spent every Saturday from the age of ten at the New England Conservatory Preparatory Division, taking lessons, performing chamber music, and attending composition seminars and improvisation classes. Her hard work and dedication led to performances both at the NEC Preparatory Division and elsewhere. A highlight of her early musical career was the performance of one of her compositions by the Boston Symphony Orchestra and the Boston Pops when she was twelve. In the realm of service, Julia also used her music to bring happiness to others, working to teach music to children's youth groups and performing in retirement homes several times per year.

The Application and Essay

In shaping her application, Julia centered her approach on her interests in music. She stressed her musical interests as much as she possibly could in the application. In order to enhance her application, she included supplementary materials in the form of a CD of her work and musical scores of her compositions.

During high school, Julia volunteered with the Conservatory Lab Charter School, which is affiliated with the New England Conservatory of Music. The school is geared toward giving underprivileged children in kindergarten through fifth grade the opportunity to be exposed to music. For three years, Julia spent time helping out in children's music classes, talking to them about music and composing two pieces that the whole school performed. She collaborated with a poet and set the words to music; then the children played violins, recorders, and sang.

In her essay, Julia chose to write about this experience. "I wrote about what I had learned through the experience, how great it was to see the excitement of these children, how it made me realize how fortunate I was to have had exposure to music and to have had lessons my whole life. I wrote about how happy the children were when they all came and made music together, how this made me realize how important music is in children's environments." Julia's college counselors at her high school and her parents read the essay and offered suggestions. Julia also chose to submit a supplementary essay on her other musical endeavors.

Contacts and Connections

Before coming to Harvard, Julia knew a number of students because quite a few people from her high school had attended Harvard and others whom she knew through her musical activities had also matriculated. Her high school composition teacher was affiliated with Harvard, and she had also met other people in the music department and says, "I think it helped me—knowing musicians who were already at Harvard. And it made me know what it was like to be a musician at Harvard, gave me some guidance."

At Harvard

Julia is now concentrating in music and is pursuing a joint-degree program with Harvard and the New England Conservatory of Music. Her activities include the Radcliffe Choral Society, the Wind Ensemble, the Harvard Baroque Chamber Orchestra, the Harvard-Radcliffe Contemporary Music Ensemble, and the Piano Society. She is also involed with the Dunster and Lowell House Opera societies, the Harvard-Radcliffe Gilbert and Sullivan Players, and the Mather House Chamber Music Program.

The Bottom Line

Julia advises that students show how they are different from every other student who's applying. She also advises students to focus on doing things that they love instead of focusing all of their energy on *getting in*. "In my experience, students who do all of their activities solely for the sake of getting into college are not the happiest. Those students who do what they love because they love it are ultimately the most successful."

—*Megan C. Harney*

Aram Demirjian

Hometown: Lexington, MA (suburban)
High School: Public school, 450 students in graduating class
GPA: 3.7 unweighted
SAT: 720 Math, 720 Verbal
Extracurriculars: Assistant conductor and first chair cello in the orchestra, played cello in Youth Philharmonic Orchestra of the New England Conservatory, member of the choir and two a cappella groups, sports announcer for a local cable station, reporter for the school newspaper.
Summer Activities: Lexington Youth Summer Theater; Boston University Tanglewood Institute Young Artists Orchestra; staff assistant, New England Conservatory; archivist's assistant for the Lexington, Mass., archives; city tour guide, Lexington, Mass.
Awards: National Honor Society, AP Scholar.
Family Background and Education: Aram's father attended the American University in Beirut and got his Ph.D. from MIT. His mother went to Brandeis.
Nationality/Ethnicity: Armenian-American
College Acceptances: Harvard (deferred early and accepted regular admission), Amherst, Georgetown, University of Virginia, McGill (Canada), Boston College, Tufts, Connecticut College
College Rejections: Yale, Brown

When Aram Demirjian applied to Harvard, his musical proclivity could hardly have gone unnoticed by the admissions committee. Aram was a fixture on his high school orchestra, playing the cello for all four years of high school. By his junior year he held the principal cello chair, and in his senior year he served as the orchestra's assistant conductor. During those same four years he also played cello for the Youth Philharmonic Orchestra of the New England Conservatory and he was a member of his high school's choir.

High School

Aram came to Harvard from Lexington High School, which usually has several students admitted to Harvard each year. Along with these grades and his musical proficiency, Aram was also a two-year member of Lexington's student newspaper, and, also for two years, served as a sports announcer for a local cable station, broadcasting high school football and basketball games.

The Application and Essay

In selling himself to Harvard, Aram was conscious to craft a particular image of himself: "I tried to really play to my strength, which I felt was music." He says he wanted to make the admissions committee confident that he would make a positive contribution to the Harvard community. "I really tried to show how the unique quality about me was music, and that I could be an asset to the various music groups at school," he notes.

To achieve this goal, Aram did more than write his extracurricular essay about his passion for music. He also sent in an audio recording of himself playing the cello, and submitted, in addition to the traditional academic résumé, a music résumé outlining his musical accomplishments and awards.

His personal essay was not music related; instead, it was a reflection on the influence of the television character Mr. Rogers on his life. Aram came up with the idea to write about the show, which he watched religiously as a youth, during a brainstorming session. Soon afterward he sat down and "free-wrote" his essay, putting onto the page whatever came into his head. And then, over the next few weeks, "I revised and revised," Aram says. Two English teachers, his mother, and his sister all read and helped redact his essay.

Contacts and Connections

Aram's interview went very well, mostly because he was able to shift the conversation to those subjects he had the most to say about—

music and history. "I remember the interview being a great experience," Aram says, noting that the interviewer took great interest in his musical talent. Aram also says he was careful not to try to emphasize all of his strong points in the interview, but only to highlight the most important areas: "I didn't try to cover too much. Just the areas where I thought I was strongest," he says. Because so much of the interview was spent discussing music and history, Aram was able to project a much stronger image of himself than if he and the interviewer would have talked about all of Aram's subjects and extracurricular activities for an equal amount of time.

Both Aram's family and his school played strong support roles during the application process. A school guidance counselor tracked the development of his application, though Aram says his mother and sister—both of whom had been through the application process before for his sister, who was a member of the Harvard class of 2003—provided particularly vital support. Though both his parents are college educated, neither of them attended Harvard and so Aram did not receive legacy status during admissions deliberations, but the fact that his sister had previously attended Harvard surely did not hurt his cause. He also attended a local high school just a few miles from Harvard's campus.

At Harvard

Aram applied early action to Harvard but was deferred; he was later accepted during regular admissions in April. Now Aram plans to joint-concentrate in government and music. He has also extended his musical interests outside the classroom—he is a member of the Harvard-Radcliffe Orchestra as well as the university choir and the Dunster House Opera.

The Bottom Line

Aram recommends that applicants emphasize their strong points! Not everyone should try to come across as a perfectly well-rounded student. If you are particularly adept at playing a musical instrument, writing a piece of comedy, or some other task, put it everywhere in your application. Also, Aram advises students to emphasize that if you get into Harvard, you plan on joining a specific extracurricular activity that will allow you to exercise your talent—and benefit the entire campus. He also recommends sending in a sample of your work, whether it be an original comic skit you wrote or a recording of yourself playing an instrument. If you are the editor of a student publication, send in a copy of the publication. Submitting extra documents like these proves your skill to the admissions committee and gives you an advantage over another student who also claims to have the skill but who did not submit proof of his quality.

—*William C. Marra*

Gareth James Doran

Hometown: Dublin, Ireland (urban)

High School: Private all-male parochial school, 180 students in graduating class

GPA: A/B student in the top 10 percent of the class (no specific GPA available)

SAT: 690 Math, 630 Verbal

Extracurriculars: Top-ranked tennis player in Ireland, Ireland National Tennis Player (ages fourteen, sixteen, seventeen), Leinster Province Tennis Player (since the age of twelve); captain and number-one player on school tennis team. Volunteer for refugee asylum center and college radio station.

Summer Activities: Played tennis tournaments around Ireland, traveled to Morocco and Malta for six weeks total at age sixteen to play tennis.

Awards: National Tennis Champion (under fourteen, under eighteen).

Family Background and Education: His father and mother were both hardworking and taught their children discipline and a strong work ethic. Gareth has an older sister and brother; his brother was the top-ranked tennis player in Ireland as a junior and went on to captain the Harvard tennis team in 2000 and later join the pro tour. "I really admire my older brother and always wanted to follow in his footsteps. Every time he achieved, it encouraged me to work harder and achieve for myself."

Nationality/Ethnicity: Irish
College Acceptances: Harvard
College Rejections: N/A

Growing up, tennis gave Gareth a lot of confidence and focus. He was encouraged and motivated by a strong family to excel both in and out of the classroom. When applying to college, Gareth e-mailed the tennis coaches at several colleges and then went after the schools where there was a mutual interest. His top picks were Columbia, Brown, Princeton, and Harvard. Though he loved the Princeton campus, Harvard was the last school he visited and he was hooked once he went to see Harvard. "The people at Harvard were incredibly driven and this more than anything attracted me to this place."

High School

He became very driven in all of his endeavors in high school, both in the classroom and on the court. "That's a sports thing in general—they give you the extra drive. When I was playing tennis I wanted to win and when I was in school I wanted to be the very best that I could be." Although Gareth started playing tennis later than most top players, he believes it was this drive that allowed him to catch up with and ultimately triumph over his peers.

The Application and Essay

In his application, Gareth tried to focus on two things: leadership and drive. "I felt that I had worked very hard to position myself with a shot to get into Harvard and I wanted that to come across in my application." He placed particular emphasis on how tennis had developed his leadership and helped him to focus. He also tried to be creative in his answers and use his imagination to make the standard, common application more interesting to read. Finally, he added some humor to the process, as "It's always good to get a laugh out of people."

Gareth chose to focus on international affairs in his essay and wrote on the Treaty of Nice, a topic that he found particularly timely and interesting. The Nice treaty is a difficult document to read and understand, in part because it is a list of amendments to already existing documents, including the E.U. treaty itself. While the treaty deals with a number of controversial issues, including trade, new E.U. rules, and the voting power of the individual countries, the feature that received the most publicity was the admittance of ten new countries to the European Union. Gareth's essay was a political critique. He discussed the fact that Ireland, and particularly the Irish media, focused much too negatively on the new members joining an expanded European Union. Gareth felt that the xenophobic attitudes and fear that the new entrants would flood the Irish job market was hypocritical for a country such as Ireland. Ireland had benefited in economic terms by being a member of the European Union and itself had difficulty in being admitted. His essay discussed the fact that a number of political groups tried to influence the referendum on the treaty to suit their own political ends.

Contacts and Connections

Gareth was initially exposed to Harvard through his older brother, John, and cousin Joe, who were both members of the Harvard class of 2000. He visited John at college when he was twelve and had wanted to attend the college ever since. This gave him early motivation to work hard. In addition, Gareth visited Harvard as a prospective student when he was in high school and this visit further strengthened his desire to attend Harvard, as he found Harvard to be a very dynamic and exciting place. "The students I met were all very accomplished and had amazing talents that really impressed me."

At Harvard

Gareth is currently an economics concentrator in the class of 2007. He plays on the varsity tennis team and enjoys intramural basketball in his time off from academics and tennis.

The Bottom Line

When asked to provide advice for other applicants, Gareth says, "There is a lot of luck involved in the process, but being prepared allows you to take advantage of any luck that comes your way."

—*Erica K Jalli*

Zak Farkes

Hometown: Boston, MA (urban)
High School: Private School, 400 students in graduating class
GPA: 2.75
SAT: 630 Math, 630 Verbal
Extracurriculars: Captain of the baseball, football, and basketball teams.
Summer Activities: Played baseball in summer leagues and recruiting showcases.
Awards: *Boston Globe* All-Scholastic Award, MVP in baseball for the Independent Schools League.
Family Background and Education: His mother attended Boston State University and is currently an elementary school principal. His father attended Hofstra University and is currently a businessman.
Nationality/Ethnicity: White
College Acceptances: Harvard (early action)
College Rejections: None

From an early age, Zak Farkes knew that sports were his passion. At age four he was playing catch with his father. When he was nine, he began playing (and starring) in the local Little League. By the time he was a senior in high school, elite schools like Harvard, Princeton, and Yale were actively recruiting him to play baseball. Here's how Zak climbed out of Little League and into the Ivy League.

High School

Throughout high school Zak was known as "the athlete." He played varsity basketball for three years, varsity football for four years, and varsity baseball for five years (he joined the high school team while still in the eighth grade). During his junior and senior years Zak also captained each of the teams. Although neither the basketball team nor the football team experienced much success, Zak led the baseball team to the Independent School League championship three years out of four. "We won over 100 games in four years—the only team to do that in league history." Zak was also a four-time ISL all-star, a two-time Massachusetts all-star, and league MVP during his senior year. Zak was recognized as a *Boston Globe* All-Scholastic athlete and was voted his high school's best all-around athlete. "I think my whole high school career was pretty simple. I did sports during the athletic times and I did academics during the academic times."

The Application and Essay

Zak did not go into the application process with any tricks up his sleeve—he just described himself as best he could. "I wanted to emphasize who I was as a person and what I could bring as a personality to the freshman class. I just tried to be honest about why I was a good fit. If I got in I figured I'd be the type of kid who would fit in."

When Zak sat down with his high school advisor to discuss topics for his college essay, he knew that he could try a bunch of different approaches. He could write a "form" essay describing his goals in life and how Harvard would help him reach those goals, or he could write about something more personal. He ultimately decided to write about baseball. "I wanted to talk about something important and meaningful in my life," he says.

Zak completed the first draft of his essay in a few hours, while sitting at his desk. He describes that draft as "mechanical," noting the difficulty of conveying his personal thoughts on paper. With the help of his advisor, however, Zak was able to focus his thoughts and communicate the ways in which baseball was personally significant. "I likened it to playing an instrument or solving equations. It was more than a game. It was an academic experience."

When it came time to ask for letters of recommendation, Zak turned to the two teachers who he felt knew him best—his junior year English teacher and his junior year American history teacher. "Those were teachers who I had gotten close to and who inspired me the most," he says. Zak also had a keen interest in the subject matter of their classes.

Contacts and Connections

Several students from Zak's high school, which is located less than 2 miles away from Harvard's campus, enroll at Harvard every year so he knew multiple Harvard students prior to applying. Likewise, his advisor and teachers knew much about the Harvard experience. "I involved them all in my decisions," he says.

During July, after he had completed his junior year of high school, Harvard's baseball coach began actively recruiting Zak. The coach spoke with Zak and his family about the benefits of playing baseball at Harvard (and about getting an education there). Harvard required Zak to verbally agree that he would attend Harvard if accepted. He therefore had to inform other baseball scouts (from other Ivy League schools, Boston College, the University of Connecticut, and Duke, among others) that he was already committed to Harvard.

Zak had an "official visit" sponsored by the baseball team. He stayed in the dorms with members of the baseball team for three days over a weekend, so he could attend classes and hang out with other baseball players. After attending parties and living with the guys, Zak was sold. "I thought Harvard would be great."

At Harvard
Zak decided to major in English and American language and literature, drawing from his high school interests in American history and
English. He joined Harvard's varsity baseball team and in his freshman year led the team in total bases, home runs, and walks, starting all
forty-three games (he was named Ivy League Rookie of the Year). During his second year, he became Harvard's career home run leader and
was drafted to play professional baseball with the Boston Red Sox.

The Bottom Line
Zak played to his strengths in his application. Because his GPA and
scores were not stellar, he focused attention on his athletic prowess.
Once Zak got the attention of Harvard's coaches, he shrewdly fostered
those relationships.

—William L. Adams

Bong Ihn Koh
Hometown: Jeonju, South Korea (urban)
High School: Public school in Germany, 108 students in graduating class
GPA: 3.8
SAT: 720 Math, 710 Verbal
Extracurriculars: Playing cello.
Summer Activities: Performed in concerts internationally, worked in a
molecular biology lab.
Awards: First Prize in the 1997 International Competition for Young Musi-
cians, Landgraf-Von-Hessen Prize for cello, national music awards in Korea.
Family Background and Education: Bong Ihn's father completed his
undergraduate studies as a medicine major in South Korea and went on to
Cornell Medical School for postdoctoral work. His mother received a master's degree in music at a Korean university.

Nationality/Ethnicity: Korean
College Acceptances: Harvard, Yale, Stony Brook University (SUNY), Princeton
College Rejections: New York University, Columbia (wait-listed)

Bong Ihn Koh is a traveler by nature. He was born in Korea, but moved to the United States at age five when his father came to America for medical school. At age fifteen, he headed to Germany for five years to pursue his career in the instrument that is at the center of his life: the cello. An accomplished concert cellist, Bong Ihn has performed with dozens of orchestras around the world as a soloist and his music has been released on numerous CDs. His strong interest in biochemistry has also been an important part of his life. Bong Ihn says his talent in the arts is what got him into Harvard. His application strategy may be of some help to those who also have exceptional abilities in a particular field and want to craft an application that will guarantee their admittance.

High School

Bong Ihn's time in high school was spent like many of his other days in life—living and breathing everything related to the cello. He began studying the instrument at age eight and had juggled performances with academics since that time. He focused all of his time and resources on his love for music, and says he didn't have any time to participate in extracurricular activities at his German high school.

When Bong Ihn arrived in Lübeck, Germany, at the age of fifteen, he did not know a single word of German. His first year of high school was spent at a German high school, where he was forced to learn the language rapidly in what he now refers to as a "crash course." After his first year ended, he transferred to an American school in Berlin and faced new challenges trying to make time for both school and cello. "I always had to think ahead and always divided my life into two," he says. During this time, Bong Ihn learned some lessons he says proved vital for his future success. "I learned how to study and practice very efficiently," he says, adding that he would often sacrifice sleep for practice. Bong Ihn took an extra year to graduate from high school partly because of these challenges that he encountered.

The Application and Essay

When Bong Ihn began to consider where he would apply for college, he guessed that his music-heavy résumé might place him in a music conservatory or another arts specialty school. Nevertheless, he knew he wanted a place where he could study biochemistry in conjunction with the cello. He applied to Harvard because "it offered a great environment for musicians who wanted to pursue other academic interests." He had heard about the college's molecular biology program and research facilities from his father, who runs a lab in Korea, and decided to take a shot at getting in.

In his application, Bong Ihn tried to emphasize his dedication to the arts above everything else. He listed his cello playing as his sole extracurricular activity and opted to include a musical résumé as a supplement to his application, detailing his awards and previous concert engagements. He also submitted a tape of a cello performance and recommendation letters from a few famous violinists and cellists whom he knew.

For his main essay, Bong Ihn chose to write about a dilemma he faced in trying to balance his music career with his academic requirements. At one point in his senior year, he was scheduled to perform two cello concerts over the course of two days. But he was also planning to take the SAT just a few days prior to his concerts. "That was the real test for me in terms of knowing whether I could pursue my dream of becoming both a molecular biologist and a concert cellist," he says. This scheduling quagmire proved to be a turning point in Bong Ihn's life, and he tried to convey this in his essay. It was at this moment that Bong Ihn realized he wanted to live a life of both music and academia. "I wanted to pursue cello and science and that's why I wanted to come to Harvard," he says.

During the writing process, he recalls having his European history teacher's wife read over his essay. He chose to focus his second essay on his experiences as a cellist and how the instrument had made such an impact on his own character and personality.

Contacts and Connections

Even though he spent his high school years on the other side of the Atlantic Ocean, Bong Ihn says he still had connections to Harvard. A cello teacher and Harvard graduate he knew contacted a Harvard music professor to notify him that Bong Ihn was considering applying to the college. Bong Ihn says that direct connection may have given him an edge in the application process.

At Harvard

Despite a hectic schedule, Bong Ihn says he has been able to keep up his cello work, although not to the degree that he would like. He still juggles academia with concert engagements and practice, which consume most of his free time. In the academic arena, Bong Ihn says he likes the extensive resources that Harvard offers. "It's so unlimited," he says. He is also enjoying taking science courses as a biochemical sciences major. Recently, he enrolled in Harvard's joint-degree program with the New England Conservatory, which will allow him to earn a master's in music and a bachelor's degree from Harvard in five years.

The Bottom Line

Bong Ihn says that as an applicant, you should "spend a lot of time thinking about what you really want much farther down the road after college." He recommends setting life goals and dreams, and then deciding whether a particular college will help in reaching those dreams. For applicants trying to decide between two interests, Bong Ihn says he thinks deliberation is really the best way to make a decision. "I would really think through why you want to do both and try to express that in your application," he says. "Try to find the link between those two fields and why that link is so important to you."

—*Javier C. Hernandez*

Emily Lucas

Hometown: Cold Spring Harbor, NY (suburban)
High School: Public school, 170 students in graduating class
GPA: 4.3
SAT: 710 Math, 800 Verbal
Extracurriculars: Class president; varsity track, lacrosse, and soccer; National Honor Society; president of Spanish club; Thanksgiving Day food drive organizer.
Summer Activities: Worked as a lifeguard, taught swimming lessons, and played lacrosse on a travel team.
Awards: AP Scholar, All-Conference in Lacrosse.
Family Background and Education: Both of her parents are college-educated.
Nationality/Ethnicity: White
College Acceptances: Harvard (deferred, then accepted), Stanford
College Rejection: Yale

About getting into Harvard, Emily Lucas says, "My hook was sports. Definitely." She was recruited to Harvard to play lacrosse, and was in constant contact with the lacrosse coach throughout the application process. But Emily insists that in contrast to the other schools that recruited her—including Stanford—"Harvard definitely made you work" to get in. Her "lax" skills alone weren't enough to guarantee her a spot at Harvard—she had to prove her academic worth as well. And there is

reason to believe her: Emily's early application to Harvard was initially deferred, and she was only admitted after further deliberation by
the admissions committee.

High School

Most of Emily's extracurricular activity centered on athletics. In addition to the twelve varsity letters she earned at Cold Spring Harbor,
during her junior and senior years she was a member of a lacrosse
travel team that competed in tournaments up and down the East
Coast. Her senior year she was voted All-Conference in Lacrosse and
was invited to represent New York state at a national tournament in
which the best players from each state compete against each other. In
track, she was voted All-Conference her junior year and All-County
her senior year.

Emily brought to the table not only excellent lacrosse skill but also
a strong academic track record. She also had several community service projects on her résumé. Her junior year she started a club designed to expose underprivileged youths to positive role models. She
also organized a Thanksgiving Day food drive and was a candy striper
at a local hospital. Her non-service extracurricular activities included
her post as class president and a membership in CSH's Spanish club,
of which she was president her senior year.

The Application and Essay

In bringing her accomplishments together into one application, Emily
says that because she knew she was looked at as a potential lacrosse
recruit, she was conscious to stress her athletic ability. She made her
application "very professional-looking," she says, including extensive
athletics and activities résumés that ran several pages and included a
paragraph explaining the nature and breadth of her contribution to
each activity.

With the application she submitted the two required essays (a personal statement and an extracurricular essay) and a third essay—a
graded paper written for an English class—that was unsolicited. Her

personal statement was a reflection on how she learned to stop being a perfectionist. "It was about how I learned to give myself a break in high school," she says. "The main thing was learning to love my flaws." Though she wrote the first draft of the essay in her first sitting, "the finished product looked a little bit but not entirely like how it started," she says. Her parents, an older sister, and an English teacher all read the essay and helped Emily in the editing process.

Contacts and Connections

Emily calls the final part of her application—the interview—a great success: "I really got along well with the guy who interviewed me. It was a good conversation. It wasn't like you were on edge."

At Harvard

Emily was ultimately admitted to Harvard, though only after her early action application was deferred. Emily's life still revolves around sports and books: She plays midfield for the women's lacrosse team and, in the classroom, she is a government concentrator who hopes to eventually work in media communications.

The Bottom Line

Emily recommends that if you are an athlete, either recruited or hoping to walk on, make sure you are in constant contact with the coach throughout the admissions process. Communication is key. You will want to let the coach know how sure you are of wanting to attend Harvard so that she will know whether or not to red-flag your application for the admissions committee. But in a situation where you are being recruited, it is not necessarily the best strategy to emphasize in your application only your athletic ability. Harvard and other elite universities apply strict academic and extracurricular standards to athletic recruits. If you prove that you are a student as well as an athlete, or that you are involved in extracurricular activities other than sports, you will put the admissions committee at much greater ease as they review your application. They answer not only to the coach, but also to their own strict standards, and if you can satisfy them on both fronts, you will greatly increase your chances of being accepted.

—*William C. Marra*

Aliaa Remtilla

Hometown: Vancouver, British Columbia (urban)

High School: Private all-female school, about 75 students in graduating class

GPA: 4.0

SAT: 710 Math, 700 Verbal

Extracurriculars: In field hockey, reserve player for junior national team in field hockey; member of provincial team; local team coach and referee. Video club captain, Duke of Edinburgh Program (community service and athletic program), multicultural club member, library assistant, peer tutor, volunteer at local mosque.

Summer Activities: Played field hockey for provincial teams and took part in national field hockey championships and coached goalkeepers. Also helped out at her father's accounting business and took extra courses, including extra academics and a modeling course.

Awards: Techno-Olympian (science competition).

Family Background and Education: Her grandparents were initially from India and later immigrated to Tanzania. Both of her parents emigrated from Tanzania to Vancouver. No one from her family had gone to any Ivy League school. Her mother stayed at home, and her father started his own accounting business.

Nationality/Ethnicity: Indian/Ismaili Muslim. (Her family adheres to the teachings of Aga Khan, and since Khan graduated from Harvard, her parents were familiar with the college and wanted her to attend.)

College Acceptances: Harvard (early admission)

College Rejections: None (She rescinded applications to Princeton and Stanford when admitted early to Harvard.)

Aliaa has played field hockey since seventh grade and the following year she switched positions to goalie, which she has played ever since. Her senior year of high school, Aliaa played on thirteen different field hockey teams. "There was this girl who had played field hockey at my high school, was on the Canadian National team, and had gone to Princeton, who was my hero. Because of her, I really, really wanted to go there initially. The summer before my senior year my dad and I flew down to Harvard and Princeton to see the campuses—I fell in love with Harvard as soon as I saw it and felt no connection at all with Princeton."

High School

In high school, Aliaa combined her passions for field hockey and the arts. She considers herself an individual and is proud of not conforming to what could be considered a "catty" environment of an all-girls school. While field hockey was certainly her main passion, she remained actively involved in the community as well.

The Application and Essay

Aliaa's application was a combination of her loves for field hockey and film. She wanted to stress both her athletic and her artistic sides to show she could contribute both in the classroom and on the field. Thus, she sent a video of clips from her field hockey games as well as a film she had made advertising her high school. The tone of the application was very confident. She stressed hard work and determination and wanted the application to say, "I work hard to get what I want and what I want is to get into Harvard."

Aliaa's essay was "an extended metaphor about combing my hair." It was meant to be quite funny as it described how she would comb her hair wishing she was a Pert Plus model. Basically, it related combing her hair to combing away all of her problems. She wrote that you comb your hair and try to get out all of the tangles but you can never really get rid of all of them. She related this example to how she went to an all-girls school that could be quite catty and judgmental at times, and how she felt that the girls all tried to "comb out" all of their own flaws in order to be perceived as "perfect." She also related this to work and how there is always more work to be done and one must go the extra mile to get what he or she wants.

Contacts and Connections

While visiting Harvard with her parents, Aliaa went to a meeting where she asked an admissions officer a question about SAT scores, and it turned out that he happened to be the Vancouver admissions officer. They had a long conversation on her background and he told her that he had heard the field hockey coach needed a goalie. Aliaa then went to watch the team and they asked about her grades and SAT scores and thought she was a strong prospect. There was no formal recruiting process through her high school, since no athletes had gone through recruiting before her, so she took her time making a highlight film while the Harvard coach was desperately trying to get ahold of her so she could meet the early application deadline. The Harvard coaches wanted her to visit campus again, but she was busy playing field hockey, so she talked to the coaches over the phone from home and e-mailed with her future teammates until she heard she had been formally admitted.

At Harvard

At Harvard, Aliaa was a visual and environmental studies concentrator. She notes, "My life is field hockey and film." She was the varsity goalie for the field hockey team and won the Ivy League Championship her senior year. To maintain her goalie skills in the off-season, she also played junior varsity ice hockey, and participated in intramural crew as well. In addition to her athletics, Aliaa worked at the athletic facilities seven to eight hours each week during the school year.

The Bottom Line

Aliaa recommends pursuing a few key goals, whatever your approach: "I guess the main thing is to study smart so that you get decent grades but that so you also have time to do other activities; try to find a balance. I also think that passion is really important—it's vital to be passionate about at least one non-academic pursuit, but it's even more important to be able to translate/transcribe that passion into your application so that the admissions officers can see it. Try to use the different aspects of the application that you submit to give the school a complete view of you as a person, highlighting your fortes." She also recommends firsthand experience, because "if you're at all an instinctual person, you'll just know whether or not the place is right for you." For fellow athletes, she says, "it's a good idea to participate in the summer camps offered by the school in your sport. A few of my teammates from obscure parts of the country were recruited through coming to Harvard field hockey summer camps that are run by my coaches."

—Erica K. Jalli

Mary C. Serdakowski

Hometown: Richmond, RI (rural)

High School: Public school, about 400 students in graduating class

GPA: 3.77

SAT: 720 Math, 570 Verbal

Extracurriculars: Varsity track and field captain, field hockey team captain, class council member.

Summer Activities: Competed in the state, regional, and national Junior Olympic meets; took summer school classes at the University of Rhode Island; attended a local music camp; worked at the University of Rhode Island–Bay Campus as a laboratory assistant and Web page designer; worked at Bradford Soap Works (West Warwick, Rhode Island) as a laboratory assistant.

Awards: *Providence Journal* Female Scholar Athlete, Rhode Island Athletic Administration Association Female Scholar Athlete, Bausch and Lomb Award, four-time New England Champion (track and field), nine-time Rhode Island State Champion (track and field), four state records.

Family Background/Education: Her mother is the Assistant Dean of Undergraduate Admissions at University of Rhode Island; her father is a chemical engineer, computer programmer, and entrepreneur, as well as the founder of Autosoft Systems.
Nationality/Ethnicity: White
College Acceptances: Harvard, Dartmouth, Notre Dame, Georgia Tech, Vanderbilt, Bucknell, Lafayette, University of Rhode Island
College Rejections: Yale, Duke

From rural Richmond, Rhode Island, Mary Serdakowski attended Chariho Regional High School, where she was a star track and field athlete and field hockey player. While investing much of her energy in these athletic pursuits, she still managed to be valedictorian of her class, and her success earned her a spot as the first person from her high school to matriculate at Harvard.

High School

In high school, Mary quickly showed her prowess both in the classroom and on the field. She excelled in chemistry, which gained her an award upon graduation. From her first day in high school, she was on the track and field team, and by the end of her tenure, she was setting school and state records. Even with much of her time dedicated to sports and academics, Mary found time to be a member of her class council during her junior and senior years, and she was a church acolyte outside of school.

The Application and Essay

Mary crafted her application to emphasize that she was more than the average athlete. She didn't want to fit a mold. "[Sports] was one thing I excelled in, but I had to make sure that I showed them that I was well-balanced." While flattered by the fact that she was recruited by a number of Division I athletic schools, Mary knew that she was also academically inclined and a participant in her school and town community. Moreover, if she wanted to get into the nation's top schools, she had to be more than just an athletic recruit—she needed to promote her other activities. She also was careful to mention the fact that she intended to be an engineering major. Mary believes that this may have helped her, as some schools are more interested in women who want to study the hard sciences.

Even though she wanted to show that she was more than just an athlete, Mary found herself writing her personal essay about her experience running indoor track freshman year. That year, her school did not provide funding for the team, so Mary had to compete as an individual. Her piece conveyed that she is self-driven and persistent, as she had to run and practice alone, while getting people to help her with transportation and paying for insurance to allow her to compete. This essay came easily to Mary, as running was such a big part of her life. She felt that this story conveyed many other positive qualities about her. She originally wrote the essay on her own, and gave her drafts to her parents and a college admissions counselor who was helping her. They gave her editing tips to improve her essay.

Contacts and Connections

Mary says that she knew no one with a connection to Harvard when she applied. She applied because a Myers-Briggs personality test told her that Harvard would be a good fit, as did her college counselor. The only person that she met other than her interviewers was the track coach. She just wanted to let him know that she was applying. Although other schools were recruiting her for track and field, she was not being recruited by Harvard.

At Harvard

Mary is studying environmental science and engineering and she's still a varsity track runner for both indoor and outdoor competitions. She also works for Dorm Crew (the dorm cleaning service), where she is currently a cleanup captain. Mary is involved in the community at Harvard, and she's the alumni representative for her Residential House Committee.

The Bottom Line

Mary's application shows that someone who is a star athlete can (or may have to) be more than just that. While some schools will recruit you for a sport and relax the admissions requirements, it's much harder to get this treatment at the nation's elite colleges. As an applicant, you have to be prepared to get in on your own merits and on the basis of your multifaceted high school résumé.

—Nicholas A. Molina

Strategy 2: Be Passionate

One tends to conceive of the college application process as a sober and serious matter. But colleges are not looking for automatons who plow through the requisite tests and extracurriculars—they are looking for people who love to learn and are open to new experiences. Having passion for a subject—and being able to demonstrate it in an application—is something that really distinguishes applicants. Even if passion for one issue, subject, instrument, or project means lower grades or fewer extracurriculars, the key is conveying your commitment.

Passion means different things to different people. Harvard student Bryan G. Chen says focusing on excellence chiefly in scientific fields was the key to his acceptance, while Lauren Bray says stressing a devotion to various activities in her essay and extracurricular list worked well for her. Neha Chauhan and Katherine L. Penner wrote about their specific passions and pursuits, dance and music. Above all, the applicants in this chapter emphasized their passions in their essays and applications.

So test yourself—do you fall into the category of applicants that should play up their passion for a particular subject or activity? Ask yourself the following questions. Is there one thing that has determined the course of your academic career, or one pursuit that has dominated your schedule? Do you see yourself as focused and determined? Have you excelled well beyond your peers in one area? If you answer "yes" to any of these questions, here are some ways to play up your dedication and commitment in your application:

- *Emphasize your passion in your essay and in your interview.* The facts may not speak for themselves: Admissions offices may not be able to infer from your extracurricular sheet that you love Rachmaninoff.

- *Don't be afraid to admit your focus.* Your interest in and time commitment to a particular issue or activity may have precluded other activities, and that's fine. When you have a demonstrated passion, prioritizing is necessary, and colleges understand this.
- *Ask for recommendations from people who have witnessed your passion take a concrete form.* It may be the conductor in your school orchestra, your baseball coach, or even a favorite teacher.

Colleges—including Harvard—love to fill their incoming classes with students who demonstrate significant passion and talent for just one or two things. If you have the credentials to back it up, emphasize a unique passion of yours and show the college of your choice what flavor you can add to their matriculating class.

Morgan Arenson

Hometown: New York, NY (urban)
High School: Private day school, 47 students in graduating class
GPA: 3.9
SAT: 790 Math, 750 Verbal
Extracurriculars: Ballet (five hours a day), French tutoring.
Summer Activities: Central Pennsylvania Youth Ballet Summer Intensive Program, School of American Ballet Summer Intensive Program, Miami City Ballet Summer Intensive Program, Ballet Academy East Summer Intensive Program.
Awards: National Merit Scholar, school's top academic and citizenship awards.
Family Background and Education: Both parents have B.A. degrees from MIT. Morgan's mother also has a public policy degree from the John F. Kennedy School of Government at Harvard, and her father has a J.D. from the University of Chicago.

Nationality/Ethnicity: Jewish/Southeastern European
College Acceptances: Harvard, Princeton, MIT, University of Chicago, University of Michigan
College Rejections: None

At Harvard, Morgan Arenson can be found twirling around many campus locations. A talented ballerina and arts enthusiast, she is also a dedicated scholar who, in addition to taking classes in history and philosophy, helps a professor with his research and serves on the advisory board of several student and faculty committees. A lover of Europe, and France in particular, she is an avid traveler and has spent several summers abroad. Nevertheless, Morgan's true passion is, and has been since she was twelve, ballet.

High School

In high school, Morgan spent almost as many hours a day in ballet class as she did on her academics. An advanced student at the prestigious School of American Ballet in New York City, Morgan attended the Professional Children's School, where she squeezed academic classes between professional ballet training and rehearsals. With around fifty students in each high school class, the Professional Children's School is a unique high school experience. "They treated me as if I were a professional dancer," says Morgan, but she did not shirk her academics. Ranked top in her class and the rare recipient of both the top academic and citizenship awards, she took classes at Fordham University, as well as correspondence courses at Johns Hopkins University. Of the four academic classes she took each semester, many were Advanced Placement classes.

AP Calculus may have been hard, but Morgan was used to pushing herself. Her ballet training was more than rigorous. With two, sometime three classes a day in addition to rehearsals, Morgan got more than a taste of life as a ballerina. She performed for several years in Balanchine's *Nutcracker* and a variety of other productions. She was even selected as an understudy to perform with the New York City Ballet. For that she worked not with her usual teachers but with professional choreographers. Only eighteen, Morgan lived the life of a professional dancer.

The Application and Essay

As much as she loved ballet, Morgan always knew that college was in her future. Her mother, a higher-education reporter for *The New York Times*, and her father, a New York City lawyer, were well-informed about her options. In looking for a focus for her Harvard application, ballet was the obvious choice.

Rather than write about dance alone, however, Morgan framed ballet as an example of her commitment, passion, and professionalism. She recalls, "Even though my interest was a narrow one and one that I planned to modify or move away from upon entering college, what it did speak to was my willingness to get excited about what I was doing and then pursue that seriously, taking it to a very high level." Her essay took that passion one step further as she argued that the skills she learned through ballet translated across disciplines and were evidence that she was "curious about many different things, particularly intellectual ones."

Contacts and Connections

When the time came to apply to Harvard, Morgan got in contact with a few girls at Harvard whom she knew from high school. She had also met a Harvard admissions officer when he visited her school during her senior year. Morgan did not receive any outside help on her application and worked primarily with her parents and her high school's college counselor. She enjoyed her interview at Harvard, in which she learned that the admissions officer had been involved in the arts when she was a student at Harvard. While she did not write a follow-up thank-you note, she did contact her interviewer to thank her after she was accepted.

At Harvard

The choice of where to go to college was not an easy one for Morgan. An academic and artistic star, she had many priorities to weigh and applied to, among others, Princeton, MIT, and the University of Chicago. It was only after she visited Harvard in the spring of her senior year that she was hooked on Cambridge. Pleasantly surprised by the balanced life Harvard students appeared to lead, she felt the school was for her. The fact that it had a ballet company did not hurt either. She packed her pointe shoes and has yet to put them away.

The Bottom Line

Morgan's advice to prospective applicants is to stand out. The best way to do so, she says, is to find your passion and reflect on how it makes you unique. "What admissions officers want to see most is a unique and interesting individual, in addition to all the numbers of standardized tests and grades," she says. "I tried to express what it was that made me particularly interesting and what that said about the broader mode of my worldview."

—Jessica E. Vascellaro

Lauren Bray

Hometown: Oceanside, CA (suburban)
High School: Public school, 702 students in graduating class
GAP: 4.7
SAT: 760 Math, 800 Verbal
Extracurriculars: Bassoonist for many school bands, performed in a community orchestra, member of track and soccer teams, member of an academic team, representative on local government's student commission.
Summer Activities: Toured Europe with the school's orchestra, conducted research at Davis.

Awards: Student of the year, science student of the year, award for marching band performance, National Merit Finalist, member of the California Scholarship Federation.

Family Background and Education: Lauren's parents met at Brigham Young University, where they both completed their undergraduate studies. Her father went on to get a doctorate in zoology from UC Davis, while her mother went to law school at Stanford.

Nationality/Ethnicity: White

College Acceptances: Harvard, UC San Diego, UC Davis, UC Berkeley, Pomona, Stanford, Wellesley, MIT, Caltech, Princeton (wait-listed)

College Rejections: Yale

Lauren Bray comes from the sunny suburban city of Oceanside, California, where she graduated from a large public school. She watches *The Simpsons* religiously, but also devotes a large portion of her time working for her church. The daughter of a lawyer and a *Jeopardy!* champion, Lauren is an avid bassoonist and scientist.

High School

A bassoonist since the sixth grade, Lauren says music consumed her time when she first started high school. "Band was pretty much my life by the end of my first year." She was a member of a number of school performing groups, including the marching band, wind ensemble, and percussion ensemble for all four years of high school. She was also vice president of concert band and a captain in marching band. On the side, she performed in a community orchestra for three years.

Lauren was also an enthusiastic athlete and student. "Being an athlete was a very good experience because I made friends outside of the academic setting who were people I normally wouldn't have met." She ran track for three years and played soccer for one year as a freshman. Following in the footsteps of her *Jeopardy!* champion father, Lauren was a member of the school's academic team for all four years and in her senior year was selected to represent her school in the

Science Olympiad. She also served for two years as a representative on her city government's youth commission.

The Application and Essay

Lauren concedes that she wasn't even thinking of applying to Harvard until her father suggested it to her. "I was applying to all of these other schools, and after he asked me to apply, I said 'okay,'" she admits. But although her application may have been submitted at the last minute, she paid close attention to shaping its content. She wanted to focus the application on her interests in math and science and her extracurricular involvement in music. "I tried to convey that I was really passionate in all of those areas," she says.

On the application itself, she says she tried to put "serious" activities at the top of her list of extracurricular activities. This meant that wind ensemble came before marching band, and that the time she had spent on the city's youth committee was positioned near the top because she thought the admissions committee might see it as more relevant than other activities.

For her long essay, Lauren chose to write a narrative about a childhood experience at a Girl Scout fair, where she first saw a scientist extract DNA from strawberries. "It led to me having a curiosity about stuff like science, and I thought it would nicely portray my passion for science," she says. Over the summer after her junior year, Lauren conducted independent research at UC Davis on immunology and the human liver. She related her experience as a young girl to her newfound interest in scientific research and what she planned to do in the future. "I talked about this and how biology is my favorite class out of all classes," she says.

Her second essay was nothing memorable, she says—she only remembers that she wrote on the topic of her musical talents. But she remembers having both her mother and father suggest ideas for possible topics and editing her essays throughout the process.

Contacts and Connections

Lauren's connections to Harvard were sparse at the time of her application. The only person she knew with any ties to the university was a student who had enrolled two years before her. She participated in an alumni interview in San Diego and did run into one piece of luck: her interviewer was a fellow bassoonist who had played in bands while at Harvard. "That was a really lucky coincidence," Lauren admits.

At Harvard

Lauren hasn't let go of her love for music and band in college—she is currently in the wind ensemble, pops orchestra, and pit orchestra for a musical. Lauren says her favorite part of Harvard is her roommate and the general spirit of her dorm. "I really like the variety of people and how people are both smart and funny," she says. She served as intramural representative this past year, coordinating all of the athletic events for the dorm. She has also taken an active role in her new church community at Harvard. She plans to study physics over the next few years but doesn't know yet what she will do after college.

The Bottom Line

Lauren says that students in high school should focus on doing what they are passionate about. "Don't live high school thinking only about college," she says. "If you stick with things you really care about, then it will show through on your application." She also recommends applying for scholarships—even those that may seem hard to get. "I didn't take the opportunities to apply for many scholarships, and looking back, that would have saved my family lots of money."

—*Javier C. Hernandez*

Neha Chauhan

Hometown: New York, NY (urban)
High School: Public school, 484 students in graduating class
GPA: 105.21 (100-point scale)
SAT: 720 Math, 750 Verbal
Extracurriculars: Member of dance team, public relations director of Key Club, member of marching band and concert band, member of National Honor Society, volunteer at local hospital, writer for high school literary magazine.
Summer Activities: Science research; started Alzheimer's Disease awareness organization for young people.
Awards: Intel Science Talent Search Finalist, Coca-Cola National Scholar, Discover Card Tribute Award Scholar, *USA Today* 2004 USA High School Academic Team, Tylenol Scholarship.
Family Background and Education: Neha's family moved to the United States from India before she was born. Both of her parents earned their doctorates in neuroscience at Indian universities and are currently scientists in New York City.
Nationality/Ethnicity: Indian-American
College Acceptances: Harvard, Yale, Princeton
College Rejections: None

Neha Chauhan was born into a family of scientists. Both of her parents spend their days studying autism in New York City laboratories, and it was this role model that sparked Neha's own interest in the sciences. Her fascination with Alzheimer's disease started in middle school and turned into a massive research project by the time she reached high school. But Neha's story does not end with her award-winning research: she founded a national community service organization as a sophomore in high school dedicated to helping those afflicted by Alzheimer's. In between running this organization, Neha found time for a long list of other activities, and to this day makes time for a long list of "boy band" concerts.

High School

At her Staten Island high school, Neha was a star student but also found time for an eclectic list of extracurricular activities. "I know I did a lot, but I loved what I did," she says. She spent all four years of high school doing research related to Alzheimer's disease, eventually proving in the Intel Science Talent Search that certain foods can reduce the risk of acquiring the disease. At the age of fifteen, Neha founded Teens for Alzheimer's Awareness, a not-for-profit organization affiliated with the Alzheimer's Foundation of America. For three years, Neha represented New York in the International Science and Engineering Fair and was her school's participant in the Science Olympics.

In addition to her interests in science, Neha maintains a passion for the arts. She spent all of her years in high school performing ballet, jazz, and modern dance in her school's dance team. She played flute in the marching and concert bands for three years. She was also public relations director of her school's Key Club, taught Spanish for two years to an elementary school class, and was a member of the National Honor Society, math team, and the school literary magazine.

The Application and Essay

For Neha, applying to Harvard was "just something I always aspired to do." On her application, Neha decided that her role as founder of Teens for Alzheimer's Awareness was the most important part of her life to emphasize. She prioritized the activities and awards that she won, putting those that related to her science interests on top. She also chose to emphasize her extensive list of extracurricular activities rather than her academic record. "I tried to show that I wasn't only scholastic and had good grades—that I did other things as well," she says.

Neha's main essay focused on the creation of Teens for Alzheimer's Awareness. In the essay, she began by explaining why she formed the organization: what she called the "ignorance of teens" on Alzheimer's disease. Then, she explained how she launched the project and the obstacles she faced along the way, including trying to convince some adults that her ideas were valid. "It was a huge journey of self-discovery," Neha says.

In her second essay, Neha wrote about her experiences as a dancer and musician in hopes of conveying other aspects of her character. In this essay, she showed how her life had been molded by her experiences in the arts. She explained her rise from a mere dilettante in the arts to an accomplished dancer. "Everything I ever learned in life was in a dance studio, and I tried to show that," she says. To make her application stand out, Neha structured the essay in the form of a photo album, reflecting on each "photo" as a vital stepping stone in her life journey. Neha sought feedback on her essays from her trusted English teacher and a few family members, including her sister and her mother.

Contacts and Connections

Though Neha lived only 200 miles away from Cambridge, she says she had little contact with anyone inside of Harvard's gates during the application process. She did participate in an alumni interview in New York, which she thinks probably helped put a human face on her application.

At Harvard

Neha says she loves the sense of community and diversity that Harvard offers. "It's the only place where the world's best gymnast and the national chess champion can be in one place together," she says. Neha loves her classes and says professors are "amazing." In her spare time, Neha continues to run Teens for Alzheimer's Awareness and has joined a number of leadership clubs at Harvard. She has decided to pursue a degree in economics but says she doesn't know where that will take her yet.

The Bottom Line

Neha says that the most important thing to getting into college is creativity. "Never lose your passion to dream," she says. She recommends that students make the most of their time in high school. "Really make your four years at high school count—make your mark," she says.

—Javier C. Hernandez

Bryan G. Chen

Hometown: Centerville, OH (suburban)
High school: Public school, 600 students in graduating class
GPA: 4.5
SAT: 800 Math, 800 Verbal
Extracurriculars: Captain of Science Olympiad, captain of Science Bowl, Dayton Philharmonic Youth Orchestra, JV tennis team, secretary of science club, National Honor Society, Dayton Association of Chinese-Americans.
Summer Activities: Conducted research at the local air force base and qualified for the job through the Wright Scholar program.
Awards: Top 25 on the U.S. Physics Team, second-place essay and first-place test score on the Patterson test, AP National Scholar, National Merit Scholar, semi-finalist on the Chemistry Olympiad.
Family Background and Education: His father is a computer engineer and his mother has a degree in English literature.
Nationality/Ethnicity: Taiwanese-American
College Acceptances: Harvard, Ohio State, Stanford, Caltech, Princeton, MIT
College Rejections: None

When Bryan G. Chen started his final year in high school, he had one important part of the college application process already nailed down: good grades and test scores. He also had a number of impressive activities and awards to his credit, including national recognition in science-related extracurriculars. However, his downsides were that he had not performed enough community service and that the activities he participated in were too concentrated in the science fields and did not reveal his well-rounded talents. He also felt that he had missed out by not holding a real-world occupation. "Come on, Science Bowl, that's not really job experience," he says. Yet, he certainly did have his niche and his résumé shined in the science fields.

High School

Bryan's high school activities mainly consisted of science competitions. He competed in the Science Olympiad, which is a team event where members are assigned to certain events and then face off against other high school students. The team, for which he was an elected captain, moved through the regional, state, and national competitions, and his senior year Bryan placed first in cell biology, second in astronomy, and fourth in physics lab. His junior and senior year, Bryan also participated in the National Science Bowl, which features four-person teams, head-to-head competition, and buzzers to ring in. "Junior year we went to Nationals, but we didn't do anything," says Bryan, who served as captain both years. "Senior year we did really well and got second." Junior year he scored high on the Patterson test and wrote an essay on the chemistry of sleep neurotransmitters that was good enough for a second-place finish. Bryan also took the Math and Chemistry Olympiad tests, and he took the second-round tests in Chemistry for two years. He was eligible to take the second-round test for the Biology Olympiad as well. Finally, he ranked in the Top 25 for the Physics Olympiad and was sent to a training camp at the University of Maryland junior and senior year.

Beyond science, Bryan's activities ran the gamut from sports to debate. "Freshman year I played JV tennis, and I played orchestra too, up until junior year, and then I quit," he notes, adding, "Freshman year I also tried policy debate for half the year, but I don't think I even wrote that on my college application, I just did it." His musical forays included a seat in the Dayton Philharmonic Youth Orchestra, where he played violin. Bryan also helped out at festival events for the Dayton Association of Chinese-Americans, and during the summers after his junior and senior years, he conducted research at a local air force base through the Wright scholars program. Needless to say, he took many AP classes and was a Presidential Scholar.

The Application and Essay

Not surprisingly, Bryan stressed his science credentials on his application. "I emphasized science and being well-rounded," he explains. "I dug up all sorts of stuff to show that I did everything." However, he admits that he did not have a set strategy for approaching the forms. "Of course you're going to try to make yourself look good, and I made sure I got the same activities on each application," he says, explaining that he listed the national-level events and awards first and then leadership positions next. "After that it's just random, whatever fits in that little box," he says. As for his teacher recommendations, he asked teachers that he knew well and who knew him and his extracurriculars well. He obtained a letter from one Science Olympiad coach who he did not actually have a class with, and one from another coach who happened to be his history teacher. Bryan cautions against teachers who balk at writing strong letters for students. For instance, he avoided asking one of his English teachers for a recommendation. "He made it seem like he wasn't necessarily going to write [me] a good one, so I wasn't going to take that chance."

When the discussion turned to the essay, Bryan exclaims: "Oh my God, my essay was the weakest part of my application." He says that he simply expanded on his Science Olympiad activities, which he felt did not make for a very inspired or original piece of writing. The essay, however, did have the benefit of being applicable to more than one college, which saved him some extra work and headache, and also meant that he had the opportunity to reexamine and revise the essay several times. He wrote the piece on his own, although, after some thought, he added that he might have given an early draft to a teacher for comments. Bryan concedes that he simply did not buy into the popular wisdom about the importance of writing an exceptionally creative essay. "What I had heard was, the first thing they're going to look at is your grades and test scores," he explains. "After that is your activities and what you did. I was just going to let those three things speak for me." If he had not been cut from consideration by that point, then he felt he would have a strong shot at acceptance as long as his essay was inoffensive.

Contacts and Connections

Bryan did not have any contacts at Harvard during the admissions process. "Some lady called me and wanted my Patterson test chemistry essay," he recalls. "That's the only outside, non-paper connection with Harvard." He visited the campus before he was accepted, but he did not meet with any admissions officers. Some alumni from his school had attended Harvard, but Bryan did not communicate with them.

At Harvard

Since starting college, Bryan, a physics major, has focused on his schoolwork. He also conducts research at a local laboratory. His other extracurriculars include teaching citizenship material in Boston's Chinatown and participating in intramural sports. He sums up his primary activities succinctly: "Studying for classes, hanging out, enjoying fine dining."

The Bottom Line

Bryan suggests to applicants that they maintain good grades and test scores and "do something amazing." For the science-oriented applicants, Bryan recommends that they stay aware of the opportunities to participate in science-related activities. He notes that there were many programs that he did not take advantage of, such as science fair projects, that might appeal to prospective applicants.

—*David Zhou*

Heather Charlotte Higgins

Hometown: Orange, CT (suburban)
High School: Private all-female parochial Catholic school, 100 students in graduating class
GPA: 3.7
SAT: 780 Math, 800 Verbal
Extracurriculars: Captain of math team, president of economics club, varsity tennis team, Milford Hospital volunteer, nursing home volunteer, co-president of French club.
Summer Activities: Research Science Institute (RSI) at MIT, conducting research at Massachusetts General Hospital in the Department of Neuroradiology. (Her mentor from that program, Dr. Leena Hamburg, "supported me throughout the college application process and inspired me to pursue my interest in science and medicine.")
Awards: National Merit Scholar, Harvard Book Award, Intel Science Talent Search Finalist.
Family Background and Education: Heather's family immigrated to Connecticut from Dublin, Ireland, when she was five and her older brother was fifteen. Her parents wanted to give their children access to a better education and work opportunities. Her mother was self-educated and works at Prudential in charitable remainder trusts. Her father died when Heather was in high school.
Nationality/Ethnicity: Irish-American
College Acceptances: Harvard, MIT, Dartmouth, Yale, Duke, University of Pennsylvania, Vanderbilt, Emory, New York University, Tulane
College Rejections: None

In addition to being influenced by her hardworking, immigrant background, Heather feels very strongly about the effect that community service had on her. Service was an important part of going to a Catholic high school and she greatly enjoyed giving back to the community.

"My high school really stressed giving back and feeling blessed for the opportunities we are all given." This really made her appreciate and feel lucky for the things she had.

High School

"My strong interest in science and the medical field was further emphasized in my college application by the types of extracurricular activities I chose to pursue in high school." From doing award-winning volunteer work at a local hospital to spending summer afternoons volunteering at a nursing home to tutoring students at Lauralton in math and science to captaining the school's math team, the genuine passion Heather had for civic involvement and math and science came through in her application. Moreover, she had an unusually strong drive and motivation for success in the school setting. She says, "Though my father unexpectedly died from cancer during my freshman year of high school, I worked very hard to hold on to the values he had given me growing up, particularly the importance he had always attached to excelling in an academic setting."

The Application and Essay

"On my application," Heather says, "I wanted to emphasize that I was a girl who wished to combine her passions for medicine and science. Having done some of my own research on the specific types of extracurriculars available at the different colleges, I was [also] able to explain in my application my interest in continuing to explore my interests while contributing to on-campus organizations." Heather initially wanted to be a pre-medical student who would later enter into an M.D./Ph.D. program, so she emphasized her experience in the Intel Science Competition and her humanitarianism as a hospital volunteer. She took a very straightforward approach to the application and did not provide any additional or supplemental materials.

Heather's essay was about dealing with a personal tragedy in her freshman year of high school. "My father was diagnosed with cancer

and five months later he passed away. It dramatically changed my outlook and really made me focus on the values he instilled in me."
Heather's father had taught her not to fear failure and to work hard, and
how he had shaped her life when she was young would prove to be a
very important force in her life going forward. He also taught her how to
"take a negative experience and make the best out of it by learning from
it," so she hoped to continue learning and growing to make him proud.

Contacts and Connections

Her senior year of high school, Heather had worked at a research institute at MIT where she met several counselors who were current Harvard undergraduates. These counselors helped pique her interest in
Harvard and got her excited about the opportunities the school offered.
They were very encouraging and helped give Heather a strong sense of
what college was like. Ultimately, when she had to make a decision
about which school to attend, Heather chose Harvard because she had
heard great things from the students and because she wanted a change
from her Connecticut-centric life.

At Harvard

Heather is studying biology; she participates in Women in Science at
the Radcliffe Institute; and has served as a program coordinator for
Project Health. In addition she has volunteered at Brigham and
Women's Hospital cardiac diagnostic intervention center. She participates actively in women's club tennis and intramural squash, and will
go on to work for Goldman Sachs Global Capital Markets upon commencement.

The Bottom Line

Regarding admissions strategies, Heather opines, "I think each student should market him- or herself as someone who is genuinely passionate about one thing. Looking at my peers, I think that that is what
contributed to their success in gaining admission." Whether it is music
or art or science research, you should show how you have demonstrated

your love for a particular field through work in and out of the class-room. "Also, demonstrate in the essays that you have done your research and give very specific reasons on why you would choose Harvard." You should show you have taken the extra step and that it's not just another school you are applying to, as you plan to make a real contribution.

—*Erica K. Jalli*

Matthew J. Kan

Hometown: Danville, CA (suburban)
High school: Public school, about 600 students in graduating class
GPA: 4.54
SAT: 800 Math, 740 Verbal
Extracurriculars: Concertmaster and Lawrence V. Metcalf Chair of the San Francisco Symphony Youth Orchestra, captain of the Monte Vista academic decathlon team, captain of the Monte Vista JETS team, National Honor Society, California Scholarship Federation, volunteer shift supervisor at Kaiser Permanente Medical Center.
Summer Activities: Toured with the San Francisco Symphony Youth Orchestra in Russia, Lithuania, and Ireland; then attended the Aspen Music Festival and School. Attended the Villanova Summer Research Institute to learn basic research techniques and epidemiological modeling.
Awards: Frank H. and Eva B. Buck Scholarship; AP National Scholar; IBM Thomas J. Watson Memorial Scholarship; solo violin performances with Oakland East Bay Symphony, San Francisco Classical Philharmonic, and Oakland Youth Orchestra.
Family Background and Education: Both of his parents immigrated from Taiwan after high school. His father got his electrical engineering degree at UC Berkeley as a Regents Scholar, and his Ph.D. at MIT; he is now a mechanical engineer. His mother graduated from the University of Kansas with a bachelor's degree in English. She then got a master's degree in computer science at Villanova.

Nationality/Ethnicity: Chinese-American
College Acceptances: Harvard, Yale, Princeton, Stanford, Duke, UC Berkeley
College Rejections: Caltech

When Matthew J. Kan was gearing up to apply to colleges in the fall of his senior year, he had an exceptionally strong advantage in terms of extracurriculars. He had just been named the concertmaster of the San Francisco Symphony Youth Orchestra, which is widely regarded as the premier pre-professional youth orchestra in the world. He had a strong background in science research and a passion for biological studies. His résumé also included many leadership positions in the extracurriculars that he pursued. However, his application package did not include strong athletics because most of his time was spent on his other activities.

High School
Matthew participated in a diverse variety of extracurricular activities in high school. Most prominently, he performed with the San Francisco Youth Orchestra and was the concertmaster in his senior year. "It was definitely a really formative musical experience for me because it was run by the San Francisco Symphony," he says. "Everyone is professional and it is a professional environment." He played chamber music with the San Francisco Conservatory of Music as well, and in the summer after his sophomore year he attended the Aspen Music Festival. "I started violin when I was four and piano when I was six, and I started playing in orchestra and chamber music groups when I was six," he says. In an understatement, Matthew concedes, "It was stuff I had been doing for a really long time." However, his activities extended beyond the music. He was the captain of the school academic decathlon team and participated in the Junior Engineering Technical Society (JETS) competition. His interest in medicine prompted him to volunteer at Kaiser Permanente Medical Center, and he spent the summer after his junior year at Vil-

lanova University's Summer Research Institute. "It was my first real introduction to research and theoretical modeling," says Matthew. The next summer, he conducted research at a lab at Stanford University.

The Application and Essay

Matthew remarks on the importance of choosing the right teacher for the application's required recommendations and the thought that should go into deciding whom to ask. His AP Biology teacher wrote one of his letters. "I knew going into college I was very strongly pre-med, so it was definitely good to have someone who was my teacher for two biology classes give me a strong recommendation," he says. His second letter was written by his AP Computer Science instructor, who had also taught Matthew for two years. Additionally, this instructor was also the faculty advisor for the academic decathlon and JETS and thus knew Matthew extremely well. He also requested a third letter from the resident conductor of the San Francisco Symphony, a Harvard alum. "He could write me a good recommendation because he knew all the things I was looking for at Harvard," namely the music scene and the pre-med track. On the activities portion of the form, "I just listed everything I did in order of time consumption, plus summer things," he says, adding, "I really don't think they care what order you put it in as long as you channel across your passion for your activities."

Matthew's essay topic concerned his obsession to join the San Francisco Youth Orchestra, and to get ahead after joining. "I wrote about the turning point where what I cared about was not getting in or seating, but the music and performance quality and pulling my weight with this really great team," he recalls. "My essay was one of those 'maturation' essays." The topic idea came naturally to him because music has been such a long and integral part of his life.

Not coincidentally, his supplemental essay also centered on music, this time regarding two international tours he took with the Oakland Youth Orchestra and the San Francisco Youth Orchestra, respectively. Matthew described the trips as lessons in human compassion and communication. Even when he could not speak the same language as other teenagers his age in Cuba, they could all play music that entertained and inspired the audience. Matthew's AP English teacher offered suggestions on the authenticity of the voice in the essays, and the speech and debate teacher tightened his focus. "It's really hard to condense an essay into five hundred words," Matthew says. He also ran his essays by a senior friend at Harvard who "had a lot of good advice on more nuanced things."

Contacts and Connections

His Harvard contacts included seven friends that he knew from the San Francisco Youth Orchestra who could fill him in about life on campus. The Harvard alum resident conductor was also a link to information and certainly a good asset.

At Harvard

These days, Matthew is still engaged in music and pre-med responsibilities. He is the co-assistant concertmaster and tour manager for the Harvard-Radcliffe Orchestra, and he also plays in chamber music ensembles. He volunteers at Brigham and Women's Hospital's emergency department. In the summer, he works on research at a lab, and he plans to write a senior honors thesis in biology. "Harvard has unparalleled resources," he gushes. "Harvard has one of the few labs that does three-dimensional imaging, and it lets undergrads experiment with what it is doing in introductory biology classes."

The Bottom Line

Matthew recommended that general applicants focus more on achieving their dreams and fulfilling their passions than on delving into activities just to get themselves into college. He also added that prospective applicants who are talented in music should try to participate in collaborative musical groups, be it chamber music or orchestra, which can help them demonstrate their musical prowess as well as their ability to be a team player.

—*David Zhou*

Andrew B. Malone

Hometown: Port Washington, NY (suburban)
High School: Public school, 340 students in graduating class
GPA: 4.96
SAT: 800 Math, 750 Verbal
Extracurriculars: Drama club, lead roles in five musicals, participation in twelve musicals, wrote two original one-act plays, directed two one-act plays, assistant-directed one full-length show, assisted in middle school theater program, Natural Helpers peer advising, academic decathlon, Academic Quiz Bowl, Mock Trial.
Summer Activities: Worked at a children's summer camp for theater called "AT LAST" during the day and in the evenings participated in local youth musical theater.
Awards: National Latin Exam gold medalist, Harvard Book Award, Intel semifinalist, National Merit Scholar, article published in *Long Island Historical Journal*.
Family Background and Education: An only child with divorced parents. His mother earned her B.A. at Providence College; his father earned his B.A. at Monmouth College.
Nationality/Ethnicity: White
College Acceptances: Harvard (early admission)
College Rejections: None

Andrew, who goes by the nickname Andy and describes himself as "quirky," loves to spend time with his friends, whether taking long walks, talking late into the night, or playing silly board games. A good listener, he has an intuitive understanding of others and enjoys helping people out. He is also an avid tennis fan who adores Serena Williams. In his free time, Andy is addicted to watching reality TV, especially *American Idol*, and when he is alone, he often sings to himself. After a "brief love affair with psychology" he chose to major in history and literature with a focus on America.

High School

In high school, Andy's main activity was drama; however, for him, the thrill of the theater came not from acting in front of an audience, but from the camaraderie he found there. "Theater for me was not just about performing but about being with my friends," says Andy. "Ironically, I found some of the most genuine people and majority of my valuable high school relationships there." Andy loved being able to work together with his peers to put on a show, and even wrote a few himself.

His high school had a tradition that one show every year would be student written; Andy had always loved writing and the idea of seeing his work onstage, so in his junior year he decided to submit a play—a retelling of the Greek myth of the judgment of Paris between Hera, Aphrodite, and Athena—which was eventually performed. Andy's second play, written his senior year, retold the story of Dido and Aeneas; he also co-wrote a farcical murder mystery called *Civility* whose main song was called "Everybody Ought to Sleep Together." Andy himself acted in a dozen musicals throughout his high school career, although he had no formal vocal or theater training other than the instruction he received in school. He felt motivated to succeed in theater by his drama coach, who encouraged his students to do their best at all times. Andy also participated in a peer-advising group called Natural Helpers, to which he was elected by the student body during his junior year. The group, which made presentations to classes in the high school about youth issues such as cocaine and other drug use, bullying and hazing, and academic pressure, and encouraged discussions of these topics, met twice a week. Throughout his high school career, Andy focused on activities that made him happy, not those which seemed the most likely to earn him dozens of Ivy League acceptances. He says, "I was told by some seniors freshman year not to do drama because it would not help me get into a good school and that I should do debate. I decided very early on that I was going to do what made me happy and do it in a big way."

The Application and Essay

Although Andy felt put off by Harvard's snobby reputation, he came to visit the campus during the spring of his junior year because his father forced him to. Once he arrived in Cambridge, he fell in love with the campus and its surrounding atmosphere—and was also impressed by the college's consciousness and refutation of its reputation. Over the summer, he filled out the common application, except for the essay, which he struggled with until early October. In his application, Andy emphasized his passion for theater and especially his work with children in theater; though he was advised not to, he ranked theater above his academic pursuits on the application because it meant more to him. Though not confident in his application, "I thought it was possible and that I owed it to myself to try."

Andy's application essay was an abridged version of an essay he wrote junior year for an intensive writing class he really enjoyed. The essay, which detailed his struggles with self-confidence after losing a lot of weight, showed how Andy learned to find confidence within himself instead of in his body image. Andy chose to submit the essay because he felt that his experience as a "fat kid" is a huge part of who he is; he wanted the college to see him as an individual and knew that the essay was perfect when someone told him it was "so Andy." Andy received help from his favorite English teacher, his eleventh-grade writing teacher, on the piece. He also wrote a second and optional essay about what theater meant to him. He described his difficulty trying to sing a song in rehearsal and how the cast clapped for him when he mastered it; his realization that this applause meant more to him than that of a true audience showed his love of camaraderie in theater.

Contacts and Connections

Although Andy had no connections at Harvard, he thought that his interview went very well. The interviewer arrived at their meeting place dressed casually and the two had a laid-back, forty-minute conversation that left Andy feeling comfortable with the experience. He never met his Harvard admissions officer and had no other Harvard connections.

At Harvard

Andy has become very active in Harvard S.T.A.G.E., a children's theater outreach program. He teaches theater in Boston once a week and is also the secretary for the group, for which he has designed a T-shirt and filmed and edited a video. During the fall of 2004, he performed in the Gilbert and Sullivan operetta *Pirates of Penzance*, but notes that it took a lot of his time.

The Bottom Line

For Andy, the most important part of the application was making sure that it represented him well on paper. "If your application reflects who you are and the things that are important to you," he says, "a school where you belong will appreciate those qualities that you are most proud of."

—*Anne E. Bensson*

Katherine L. Penner

Hometown: Arlington, VA (suburban)
High School: Public school, about 350 students in graduating class
GPA: 4.3
SAT: 760 Math, 760 Verbal
Extracurriculars: Ballet, National Honor Society, Fine Arts Apprentice Program, associate art editor for the school literary magazine.
Summer Activities: Intensive summer programs in ballet at Princeton Ballet School for two summers, volunteer dance program coordinator for young children. Also, Penner was one of thirty-five people in the nation chosen to attend a summer program taught by legendary ballerina Suzanne Farrell.
Awards: National Achievement Scholar.

Family Background and Education: Father attended Cornell as undergrad, Princeton for a graduate degree, and George Washington for his J.D. Her mother attended the College of Mount St. Joseph as an undergrad and George Washington for her J.D.
Nationality/Ethnicity: African-American/Caucasian (biracial)
College Acceptances: Harvard, Columbia, Cornell, Duke, Princeton, Stanford, University of Virginia, Washington University
College Rejections: The Juilliard School

Katherine L. Penner is passionate. Her passion for dance throughout high school as well as a dedication to service and a strong academic record added flair to her college applications. Her demanding dance schedule required a number of sacrifices and Kate was willing to make those sacrifices while at the same time not becoming myopic.

High School
Kate's high school experience was dominated by dance training. "By far, my number-one activity outside of school was ballet," says Kate. "I danced upward of thirty hours a week, sometimes even fifty, and that's what my life revolved around." In addition to dancing, she was also involved in numerous service programs. "With the IB Program at my high school, I did a lot of service: tutoring kids, volunteering at a literacy program as well as a summer dance program for young children," Kate says. But her life was not completely dominated by her extracurricular interests. As the vice president of the National Honor Society, an associate art editor for the school literary magazine, and diversity peer trainer, Kate was actively involved in her school community.

The Application and Essay
"When it came to writing about extracurriculars on my application, I put a truthful representation of what I did during my spare time, which was pretty much only dancing," says Kate. Despite her other involve-

ment on campus, her major time commitment was dance and she wasn't afraid to showcase that. Kate actively pursued the dance and admissions department to illustrate her prowess. "One interesting thing I did was, I had a video editor help me compile video clips of me dancing, and sent it to schools who said that their arts department would review it during the admissions process," says Kate. "It was important to me that they understand how much time and effort I put into my dancing, and that it wasn't me just prancing around in a tutu."

Because of the common theme of dance in her application, Kate also used her essay to illustrate dance's importance in her life. "I chose the 'write about a person' common application essay, and subsequently tailored it for every other school I applied to," says Kate. "I wrote about my ballet teacher, who is a close personal friend and has really taught me about more than ballet." Coming up with the idea was simple because it seemed to her to be the only motivating thing she could write about on the application. Kate wrote about what she knew. "This question just jumped out at me as something I could really write well, and relatively easily," Kate says. Kate did not solicit any help for her application essay and acknowledges the risks. "The risks didn't matter to me, I was willing to take that risk in order to keep my own voice in it," says Kate. "I had heard about applicants having tons of people proofread and tailor their essay, and I really thought that was the wrong way to go about it. I wanted the essay to be one hundred percent my own."

Contacts and Connections

Kate knew no one at Harvard. She claims that out of all of her interviews, her Harvard interview stood above the rest. "I wanted to show that I wasn't one-dimensional, that while I did one thing particularly well, I wanted to use the opportunities at Harvard to try new things," says Kate. Kate also notes that her success in her interview was due to the fact that it was more of a conversation than a formal meeting.

At Harvard

For an outspoken Democrat, Kate is often on both sides of the fence when it comes to campus issues. Finding herself aligned with a more conservative brethren in regards to the Larry Summers's debacle about women in science, she aims to master both non-partisan and partisan politics. Kate is also a member-at-large for the Harvard Democrats. Outside of the political scene Kate is a leading force in the Harvard Ballet Company.

The Bottom Line

Kate advises applicants to "use the parts of your application that aren't grades or test scores to really show your personality and something about yourself. Use the essay to let your voice be heard because there is always someone who is just as qualified on paper as you are. Don't mold yourself into whatever you think the admissions officers are looking for. Just be genuine."

—Adam P. Schneider

Strategy 3: Find the Perfect Balance

Though some applicants can boast of winning Intel science prizes or being published authors before they graduate from high school, many successful Harvard students don't have one particular area in which they excel. Rather, they try to demonstrate balance—excellent SAT scores and grades, willingness to take tough classes, and a wide range of extracurriculars. Admissions officers can't label these students as one type—an athlete, an artist, a math genius—but rather are confident that balanced applicants will be the backbone of a Harvard class once they get in, leading student groups and participating actively in the Harvard community.

Balanced students—who often play sports, write for the newspaper, play a musical instrument, participate in student clubs, do community service, and who manage to graduate at the top of their class—stand out by showing the admissions office that they can't be pinned down as an artist or an athlete but have demonstrated all-around excellence. They may not have won national debate competitions, but they were the president of the debate team and participated in half a dozen other clubs. Rather than seeking a focal point for their applications, they simply try to demonstrate well-roundedness. This isn't just extracurricular, though—many of the students profiled in this chapter took their interests in academics beyond school, studying economics at the local university or attending summer programs in math.

If you do not have one particular talent, but have done well at most of what you have tried at high school, balance may be the aspect you should emphasize in your applications. Students who fit this profile should be at the top of their class in most academic areas and should hold leadership positions at their school; they should also be involved with the community.

- *When emphasizing your activities, don't gloss over any.* You don't want to give the impression that you joined tons of clubs to pad your résumé but were not serious about them. Make sure you explain why each was meaningful.
- *Send in peripheral materials with your application.* If you have a copy of the school newspaper you edited or wrote for, a photo you took, or anything you think might convey the importance of your extracurricular activities, it can't hurt the application.
- *Take as many AP classes as you can.* The admissions office wants to see that you've challenged yourself academically in all areas.
- *Take more than the required number of SAT subject tests.* If you're not a star at math or physics, these tests can help prove that you're an all-around academic overachiever.

Siobhan P. Connolly

Hometown: Walpole, MA (suburban)
High School: Public school, 275 students in graduating class
GPA: 3.4 (estimated)
SAT: 720 Math, 760 Verbal
Extracurriculars: Student council vice president, dance at Walpole Dance Center, varsity field hockey captain, peer ministry (community service) at local church, school newspaper, Irish step dancing at the Harney Academy, National Honor Society.
Summer Activities: N/A
Awards: Homecoming queen, senior superlative—Best All Around, Bay State League All-Star in field hockey, *Daily Transcript* All-Star, Bay State Games 2003 and 2004.
Family Background and Education: Her father got his B.A. in administration from Boston State College, and her mother has a B.S.N. from

Northeastern, an M.S.N. from UMass Boston, and is a certified family nurse practitioner.

Nationality/Ethnicity: Irish-American
College Acceptances: Harvard, Middlebury, Northeastern, Stonehill, St. Anselm's, American University
College Rejections: Dartmouth, Georgetown, Holy Cross (wait-listed)

Siobhan P. Connolly, a Massachusetts native, is truly a renaissance woman. In high school Siobhan participated in numerous activities, including varsity field hockey, dance at the Walpole Dance Center, Irish step dancing, student council, and National Honor Society, while all the time working at a local restaurant and maintaining a very competitive GPA.

High School

Although many students admitted to Harvard have lists of activities that go on for pages, Siobhan's is relatively short. However, her activities list is a textbook case of quality trumping quantity. "There were a lot of clubs and activities that my high school offered so, in my freshman year, I tried to do as many as possible just to get a feel of what my school had to offer," Siobhan says. However, the key to her success was setting priorities. "After freshman year I was able to focus on the ones that really interested me, like student council," Siobhan notes. In student council, Siobhan served as vice president. On the field, Siobhan was a varsity athlete with the field hockey team, and she was captain during her senior year. She also pointed to the large amount of community service that she did with the National Honor Society as a major time commitment. In addition to having held major leadership roles within her school, Siobhan had danced for a remarkable sixteen years with the Walpole Dance Center.

The Application and Essay

When the time came for college applications, Siobhan approached the process with a competitive attitude in mind. "Everyone told me that I needed to try and sell myself on my college applications," she says. "I answered all of the questions with that in mind, because I didn't want to sell myself short. I consider myself a pretty well-rounded person and just hoped that that would come through on my applications." As a result, Siobhan felt that the most important component of her application was the extracurricular activity résumé, since it enabled her to show the admissions staff her ability to manage her time well and excel simultaneously.

In her essay, Siobhan wrote about a subject close to her heart: her family. "I felt that my family was, and still is, something that has shaped me in every aspect of my life—my goals, my personality, and my general outlook," she says. "I thought that my experience as the oldest child in a family of eight was unique." With such a familiar subject it only took Siobhan about a week of working on and off during September of her senior year to finish her essay. She also received minimal help from her mom and her English teacher.

Contacts and Connections

During her interview Siobhan focused on being herself. As such, it was easy for her to enjoy talking to her interviewer about himself and his experience at Harvard. In the end, she was left with the feeling that the interview went off without any major problems. However, she cautions, "I don't really know how important the interview was."

At the beginning of the application process, Siobhan decided that she was interested in pursuing field hockey in college and, in mid-November, contacted the field hockey coaches at Harvard to express her interest. "We talked about my application," she admits, "but I had to wait until April to hear about a decision with the rest of the regular decision applicants."

At Harvard

Siobhan continues her field hockey career, is involved with the Christian group Athletes in Action, and hopes to resume dancing soon. She plans on concentrating in government.

The Bottom Line

"[Harvard] get[s] a lot of interested athletes, so it's really best for the player to contact the coach and let them know that you are out there," Siobhan notes about her experience. Siobhan's case shows that her well-rounded application and her above-average skills would have been nothing without personal contact with the coaches at Harvard, which she initiated herself.

—Alexander H. Greeley

Nicole K. Efron

Hometown: Bethesda, MD (suburban)
High School: Private all-female academy, 75 students in graduating class
GPA: 4.0
SAT: 800 Math, 760 Verbal
Extracurriculars: Swim team, captain of trivia team, chorale, student government.
Summer Activities: Volunteered at Columbia Lighthouse for the Blind, a summer camp for blind children; traveled to France for a month with a cultural and language immersion program; volunteered at Sibley Memorial Hospital; and worked as a waitress in a local restaurant.
Awards: National Merit Scholar, First Prize American Math League, prizes in *le Grand Concours* (National French Test).
Family Background and Education: She's an only child; her mother attended college in Australia and earned a Ph.D. in economics in the United States and her father attended college and earned an M.B.A.
Nationality/Ethnicity: Thai-American

College Acceptances: Harvard
College Rejections: None

Petite, energetic, and boasting an unruly short haircut, Nicole K. Efron has an infectious smile and an unusual sense of humor. She loves learning and has a wide academic palate that includes Chinese, economics, and chemistry. A morning person with a flair for organization, Nicole has a spunky sense of style, including her love of '80s music, her neon-green tennis sneakers, and cartoon T-shirts. In her free time, Nicole enjoys hanging out with her friends, frolicking in the leaves or the snow, season permitting, and watching episodes of *Friends* or *The Simpsons*.

High School

Though she would not describe herself as a natural athlete, Nicole's favorite activity in high school was swimming. She joined the team her junior year and swam the 500m and 200m freestyle both her junior and senior year. "I started off as one of the slowest on the team," Nicole says. She began slowly, learning basic techniques such as diving and flip turns, but every new accomplishment made her feel proud. Nicole turned her weakness into an advantage by watching the other, better swimmers and learning what she needed to do to succeed on the team. She dedicated extra time after practice to improve her skills and times, with the support of her coaches, who were very enthusiastic. During the summer after her junior year, she joined one of her coaches' recreational teams to continue practicing the sport. That fall, she asked the coach to write one of her college recommendations.

In addition to swimming, Nicole also participated on her high school's trivia team and sang the alto part in chorale. She joined the trivia team her freshman year, and though it was not offered her sophomore year, persisted during her last two years of high school and became captain when she was a senior. She was also the treasurer of her student government during her sophomore and junior year, which allowed her to work with her school's financial office. The position was not available her senior year.

The Application and Essay

Nicole decided to apply to Harvard early decision three weeks before the application was due during the fall of her senior year. "My goal in the application, as in life, is balance," she said, noting that this was also the philosophy of her school. She knew she did not have a legacy or particular strong point to rely on, and so built her application to showcase her well-rounded interests as well as her academic achievements, which included an independent chemistry project her senior year. Titled "The Impact of Land Use on Water Quality in Rock Creek Park," her project was self-designed, as highlighted in her application by a recommendation written by Nicole's advisor, who was also her chemistry and homeroom teacher. Along with her essay, it became a focal point of her application.

Nicole chose to write her essay on one of the sample topics on the common application form asking her to describe an inspirational historical or fictional character that had had an impact on her life. She wrote about Babe the Pig because she had to watch the movie several times while home sick for a few days during her senior year. After a while, the sappy quotes got stuck in her head, and Nicole began to relate the moral of the movie—that Babe overcomes several obstacles, including his own natural disadvantages, to achieve his dream of becoming a sheep-herding pig—to her own swimming success story. The idea reinvigorated her thought process—she had been writing essays about swimming for the previous week with little success—and she wrote the rough draft of her essay in a few hours one afternoon. It went through several revisions, and Nicole credits her father and guidance counselor with helping her to be more concise.

Contacts and Connections

After sending in her application, Nicole was interviewed by a Harvard alumnus in Washington, D.C. She felt very nervous about the interview and was worried afterward that she had presented herself poorly. She never met her Harvard admissions representative and had no other Harvard connections.

At Harvard

Nicole was admitted to Harvard early and did not apply to any other college, as her high school has a policy that students who are admitted early must attend that college. A member of the class of 2008, she spent her freshman year trying various academic activities such as producing a play, tutoring underprivileged children in Dorchester, and tae kwon do. She has also discovered a love of the Chinese language and plans to attend the Harvard Summer School in Beijing during the summer of 2005. In her free time, she continues to swim recreationally.

The Bottom Line

Nicole believes that the most important thing to do in any application is to show the college one's potential—"what makes you, personally, valuable to them." In her opinion, the ideal application would show the college why the applicant would be an interesting addition to campus life. "Play to your strengths," she says.

—Anne E. Bensson

Jordan S. Fox

Hometown: Linwood, NJ (suburban)
High School: Public school, about 400 students in graduating class
GPA: 4.0
SAT: 790 Math, 710 Verbal
Extracurriculars: Varsity soccer and tennis, president of branch of National Honor Society, president of student council
Summer Activities: "Every summer in high school I went to sleepaway camp and, one summer, I went on a tour of Europe with my camp."

Awards: National Merit Scholar.

Family Background and Education: Both of his parents went to University of Pennsylvania. His dad is a doctor and his mom is "mostly a homemaker, although she does teach music part-time."

Nationality/Ethnicity: White

College Acceptances: Harvard, Rutgers, New York University, Boston University

College Rejections: None

Jordan's strongest assets are his dedication and charisma. When a problem needs to be solved there is no one else his friends would rather have on their side. He will take the hardest classes and do whatever he has to in order to succeed. Of medium height and a solidly muscular build, this sophomore combines his tenacity with an easy likability that instantly relaxes those around him. But don't let his everyguy attitude fool you; underneath his blithe demeanor is a passionate intelligence. Jordan is the model of the personable, well-rounded applicant.

High School

Jordan's high school days are indicative of his nature as an extroverted and impressive regular guy. As he remembers those years, "I spent most of my time studying, playing sports, doing clubs, and hanging out." The "clubs" included opportunities to give back to his school community and the local community: "I was president of my junior and senior class, and I was president of National Honor Society in my school, which involved organizing a lot of community service activities." Much of the rest of Jordan's attention was taken up with athletics: "I played JV soccer and tennis for a bunch of years, and when I wasn't doing a sport went to the gym about four to five days a week." A light academic load allowed Jordan some time to relax in the midst of this heavy extracurricular load. He remembers that "I didn't usually have more than an hour of homework a night, so I spent the remainder of the night going out to eat with my friends, watching TV."

The Application and Essay

Although Jordan's high school years sound like the quotidian life of an average student at the average American high school, or at least those portrayed in pop culture, Jordan had a tremendous education and direction as to the right way to package his interests. He remembers that "in my application, I tried to emphasize both my math and verbal—basically history—strengths, and also my leadership." Jordan is typically modest about this final skill, calling it "bullshit."

Jordan's "essay was about my name, where it came from, and what it means to me. Mostly it dealt with the fact that my Hebrew name [Ya'akov] means "heal" and how I see myself as supporting the legacy of my parents and grandparents and so on, who, in turn, have given me my name." How did he choose this topic? When it came time to write his actual essay, Jordan decided to take inspiration from a previous work of his. "It was actually an assignment for my sophomore English class that I unearthed senior year and revised. My senior year English teacher helped me a lot with it."

Contacts and Connections

And his strategy worked. In the end, Jordan's extracurricular schedule, his GPA, and his application put him over the top even without any Harvard connections. The only interaction Jordan had with Harvard people was his interview. "I had an interview with an alumnus in New Jersey. It went well and he said he would recommend me, but I don't know how much that helped." Jordan clearly feels that his strength was his application and his well-rounded capabilities.

At Harvard

Now that he's here, Jordan is taking it slower and enjoying his interpersonal relationships. Much of his time is spent with his friends and pursuing his studies with the same level of dedication he always showed. "At Harvard, I spend most of my time either working or hanging out." In other words, he doesn't pursue "all that many organized extracurricular activities."

The Bottom Line

Looking back, Jordan is certainly philosophical about his path to Harvard. Thinking about lessons for others based on his experience, he says: "Balance is definitely important, but so is commitment. Finding extracurriculars you enjoy will lead to leadership and service activities that work well to define you as a student. And remember to play a lot of Nintendo." It is a unique lesson, but one that demonstrates the laid-back personality that makes Jordan so valuable a presence at Harvard.

—*Scoop A. Wasserstein*

Jason McCoy

Hometown: San Angelo, TX (small city)
High School: Public school, 240 students in graduating class
GPA: 104.16/116
SAT: 800 Math, 710 Verbal
Extracurriculars: Student council president, vice president of orchestra, theater treasurer, Business Professionals of America (state competitor), InterAct community service, math club president, National Honor Society vice president, co-captain of Fellowship of Christian Athletes, American Legion Oratorical Contest (state competitor), Texas Honors Leadership Program, church youth group.
Summer Activities: Texas honors leadership program, Immanuel Baptist Church youth group, American Legion Boys State, and other summer work around his high school.
Awards: Hugh O'Brien Youth Leadership Conference, Rotary Youth Leadership Awards.

Family Background and Education: His mother has a high school diploma and his father has a G.E.D.
Nationality/Ethnicity: White
College Acceptances: Harvard (early action), William & Mary, New York University
College Rejections: None

Jason McCoy was born in California, but his family moved to Texas when he was ten. Jason describes his hometown as a small city, and even though Jason went to a fairly large high school, he made his presence felt in the many ways he interacted with his high school community. He participated in a number of diverse extracurricular activities and showed that he could balance them all and excel at each.

High School

In high school Jason was involved in quite a number of extracurricular activities, from student council to math club to community service organizations. While keeping up his academics, Jason thought it was important to be a part of everything that interested him. Some of his extracurriculars were connected to his academic strengths, but many others, such as orchestra and theater, were not. More important, Jason did not limit himself to the activities that were offered by his high school. He succeeded in seeking out meaningful activities offered by his church and his local Rotary club. His persistence in finding these groups, his dedication, and the fact that his interests were varied were certainly all assets to Jason's application.

The Application and Essay

Jason only used the common application to apply to the schools that he wanted to attend. He says that he did not have a focal point that he emphasized on his application other than "well-roundedness." He says, "I just filled out the forms and answered the questions." Jason filled out his application with a broad, well-rounded image of himself in mind, because that is how he had been told to do it all through his high school career. Jason wanted the person reading his application to see him as a whole package. Overall, he wanted the application to persuade its readers that he is confident and capable through his impressive list of activities and achievements.

He wrote his essay the summer before his senior year, when he was feeling bored and had a sudden epiphany. Jason knew that he had a life plan that he would like to follow; he knew he wanted to get from where he was to the presidency of the United States and had an idea of how he thought he'd get there. He decided that it would be interesting to write a profile of his future life in reverse chronological order. He meticulously wrote about himself as president, followed by his path to the presidency and ending with himself as he was (a Harvard applicant). After finishing his application essay, he asked his English teacher to read and edit it. She gladly helped Jason work on it.

Contacts and Connections

Jason felt that he had no connections to Harvard. "As far as 'connections' and 'contacts' go, in a political or influential sense, I had none," he says. He did, however, know one person at Harvard before he applied. His counselor at American Legion Boys State was a Harvard student who encouraged him to apply.

At Harvard

Jason is planning to study psychology. He is involved in the Oak Club, the Harvard College Leadership Development Program, the Reformed Christian Fellowship, and Harvard Model Congress. He also has a part-time job fundraising for the Harvard College Fund.

The Bottom Line

Jason's application used the tried-and-true method of showing ability in a number of fields. Even in a day and age when the well-rounded applicant has been maligned, Jason showed that his involvement in sports, the arts, and the community was a winning admissions combination. It must have been his better sense of balance that separated him from other applicants who were at the top of their respective classes.

—*Nicholas A. Molina*

Muriel Payan

Hometown: Los Angeles, CA (urban)
High School: Public school, 754 students in graduating class
GPA: 4.6
SAT: 700 Math, 760 Verbal
Extracurriculars: Member of Future Business Leaders of America chapter, founder of French club, freshman mentor, peace organization organizer, competitor for academic decathlon.
Summer Activities: Interned at a local Latino community center.
Awards: First place in the Future Business Leaders of America economics division, Governor's Scholar, Kodak Young Leaders Award, Yale Book Award, National Hispanic Recognition Program Scholar.
Family Background and Education: Muriel's father—a native of India—did not attend college. Her mother completed some college in her home country of Nicaragua but never received a degree.
Nationality/Ethnicity: Hispanic Indian
College Acceptances: Harvard, UCLA, UC Santa Barbara, UC San Diego, UC Berkeley, Stanford, Yale, Columbia, University of Pennsylvania, Cornell, Princeton, Dartmouth, Brandeis, Duke, UNC Chapel Hill, Washington and Lee, Washington University, Northwestern, New York University
College Rejections: None

Muriel grew up in the heart of Los Angeles, California, raised by her Nicaraguan mother. Attending a large public high school, she always had a desire to stand out. When her senior year rolled around, she knew college would be the opportunity of a lifetime. "I wanted to apply to the best schools in the nation, including Harvard," she says. Muriel submitted nineteen applications in total, gaining acceptance to every single school she applied to. Her strategy may be of interest to those hoping to have a similar rate of admission.

High School

Muriel built up a varied list of activities during her four years in high school, balancing her interests in community service and leadership. She joined the Future Business Leaders of America at her high school as a sophomore and became the chapter's president in her senior year. As a senior, she founded her school's first-ever French club. For one year, Muriel competed on her school's academic decathlon. For three years, she was on her school's honor society and eventually became the president of the group.

Muriel also took on a number of endeavors in her local community during high school. She was a member of a student peace group for three years, tackling issues like domestic violence and sexual assault. As a senior, she mentored at-risk freshmen making the transition to high school. On the side, Muriel pursued her interest in economics by participating in a business and college preparatory program at UCLA's Anderson School of Management for two years. She also held a job as a telephone interviewer for research firms for two months.

The Application and Essay

Muriel approached her application hoping that it would turn out like a mosaic—she wanted it to reflect her diverse character in a personal way. "Basically, I kind of wanted to convey that I was diverse in what I was involved in and what I achieved to cover all of the bases," she says.

To accomplish that, Muriel placed the extracurricular activities that she considered most important to her and the ones she was most involved in at the top of her list. "I tried to diversify the activities that I was involved in," she says. The groups in which she had held leadership positions were listed first, and her list of awards was prioritized to emphasize the awards with the biggest names and most national recognition.

Muriel used her main essay to emphasize her involvement in a wide range of extracurricular activities. "I believe my academic record speaks for itself, but it does not speak for me," read the first sentence of the essay. But the essay wasn't simply a rehashing of the activities she listed on her application. Muriel used the essay to explain how her activities reflected her different academic interests and how she wasn't able to follow these ambitions as much as she would have liked with a "diluted" high school curriculum. She tied the essay together by emphasizing her strong desire to attend college. She stressed the fact that she wanted to learn more about her diverse interests, including business, economics, and history.

Her second essay focused on her experience at Casa de Pueblo, the Latino organization that she volunteered at for one summer during high school. She discussed how the projects she worked on and the people she worked with taught her about broader labor issues present in California and internationally. Muriel had a representative at UCLA read over her main essay, but other than that, she didn't receive any other feedback.

Contacts and Connections

Muriel had a few distant connections that she thinks might have helped her in gaining admission to Harvard. She signed up for an alumni interview in California and says she made a special effort to accommodate the interviewer's schedule and show general kindness toward him. "I learned that you don't argue with the interviewer, you just have to show up." Muriel says that the alumnus told her that the interview could do nothing but help her application, which made for a more relaxed interview session. Besides the interview, Muriel also asked a family friend who was a Harvard graduate to write a supplementary letter of recommendation.

At Harvard

Though Muriel has contemplated going into journalism, right now she is focused on her immediate academic future as a social studies major. She loves getting to meet new people at Harvard and says she has found the population very diverse. "It's true when they say the world comes to Harvard," she says. At Harvard, she is the activities committee representative for a Mexican-American group on campus. She has also participated in Harvard's Model Congress program and is a member of a Latina student organization.

The Bottom Line

In the end, Muriel says the key to getting accepted is how you present your application. She recommends filling the application itself with a diverse list of activities and experiences. "Colleges want to diversify their student body not just with minorities but with people of different experiences, interests, and backgrounds," she says. She also notes that applicants should spend a lot of time working on their essays and giving them a unique voice. "Be genuine in your essays because colleges are trying to get a feeling for who you are. They can tell when you're being fake," she says.

—*Javier C. Hernandez*

Zachary Rothstein

Hometown: Hanover, VT (rural)
High School: Public school, 175 students in graduating class
GPA: 3.97
SAT: 800 Math, 700 Verbal
Extracurriculars: Captain of debate team, school's student representative on the school board, representative on the High School Council (student government), member of the National Forensics Society, manager of the school chorus, director of the a cappella group, reporter for the high

school newspaper, played tennis and rowed crew, starred in two musicals, worked at the science museum, tutored middle school students.

Summer Activities: Employment at the local Montshire Museum of Science.

Awards: Various speaking awards for debate, four-year award for all-state chorus, high scorer award (for state choral audition), St. Lawrence Book Award, Chorus Award, school civic award, Presidential Scholar nominee.

Family Background and Education: Zachary's parents both went to Boston University as undergrads, where they met; his mother also got an M.F.A. in visual arts from BU, and his father went to BU Medical School.

Nationality/Ethnicity: White

College Acceptances: Harvard (early admission)

College Rejections: None

Zachary Rothstein grew up in the fresh and crisp air of rural Vermont, which helped shape his love of the outdoors. However, he says that he has a very split personality, with his more natural side loving music and the outdoors, and the other more pragmatic side drawn to law, politics, and international relations. "In my life," he says, "I strive to find a combination of these two interests."

High School

Zachary attended Hanover High School, a small, academically rigorous public school in New Hampshire near the border with Vermont. He was extremely involved in his high school community, serving as Hanover's representative on the school board. In addition, he held a leadership position in the High School Council, the governing body of the school, as well as chaired the administrative committee and the curriculum committee of the council. Other leadership activities included captain of the debate team, manager of the chorus, co-director of his school a capella group, and director of a musical. He achieved distinguished excellence in all of these activities, becoming a nationally ranked debater by his senior year of high school and participant in the all-state chorus in New Hampshire for all four years, in two of which he was the highest scoring bass. In addition, he held lead roles in *Guys and Dolls* as well as in an ambitious undertaking of *Les Misérables*. For four summers, Zachary worked at the local science museum, the Montshire, leading hands-on science activities for kids, working at the admissions desk, running snake shows and other demonstrations, and interacting with and engaging the visitors. Working at the museum was very rewarding for him, Zachary says: "I've always liked interacting with and teaching kids, and being able to get them excited about it. And I got to play with boa constrictors." Although this activity was very different from his primary interests in school, he loved the opportunity to do something different.

The Application and Essay

In his application to Harvard, Zachary tried to cover all the bases. "I was into a lot of different things," he says, "and I wanted that to show, so different parts of my application stressed different parts of my personality and strengths." He wrote two essays that were very distinct and focused on areas that his application and résumé did not emphasize. He wrote about his leadership role in the Hanover High School Council and the school board for his most significant activity statement, because he wanted to explain how important those institutions were, knowing that they were not addressed elsewhere through his essays or recommendations. His recommendations—one from his debate coach, who spoke about his passion for debate, and the other from a teacher who stressed his love of learning—strengthened the characteristics he put forth in his application.

For his college essays, Zachary wrote his main one about an annual backpacking trip he makes with his dad in the summer. The idea actually came to him extremely early, even before he was considering Harvard. The summer before his junior year, Zachary thought that writing about backpacking would be a great way to show off the more relaxed, down-to-earth aspect of his personality. The essay began with his love of being out in the woods and not having to worry about schedules and e-mails and commitments, and how great an opportunity it was for him to relax and live in the moment, something he truly values. Zachary wrote his second essay about working at the Montshire Museum, because he really wanted to talk more about this experience rather than just listing it on his résumé. "I wrote about how one day I had to crawl into an air vent to pull out a boa constrictor that escaped from its cage, and I was able to reveal another aspect of my personality," he says. The essay was funny, and so it complemented the other one well. His parents and his teacher helped Zachary edit both essays.

Contacts and Connections

Zachary did not have many contacts at Harvard, although the husband of his debate coach knew the debate coach at Harvard and wrote him an e-mail about Zachary's strength in debate. Zachary thought he might have been flagged in particular for debate, although because he was admitted early, even if he had been, it likely had no bearing on his application.

At Harvard

Zachary jumped into many different things quickly, including the policy debate team as well as Harvard-Radcliffe Collegium Musicum, a prestigious classical sixty-member mixed choir. However, according to Zachary, he "is the kind of person where everything I do must be done to an extraordinary high set of standards, and I couldn't handle doing everything." He says that because he did so much debate in high school, he wanted to try different things, which is advice that he gives to all upcoming college students. So Zachary dropped debate to pursue music, and became manager as well as tour manager for Collegium. In addition, he sings with the Chamber Singers, a subset of the Collegium Musicum, and serves on the legal research board of the Small Claims Advisory Service, a non-profit group that gives legal advice on small-claims law to indigent clients in the Boston/Cambridge area.

It is at Harvard that Zachary discovered his new passions, both academic and musical. Singing with the Collegium Musicum is the most significant experience for him at Harvard, and it is through his classes that he came to develop a love of Russian language and culture. His ambition is to attend law school, where he could study international law. In summer 2005 he plans to both study and sing in Russia.

The Bottom Line

So what does Zachary have to say about his college admission process? He offers this piece of advice: "Be original. Don't let yourself get bogged down in how to impress your admissions officer, but rather express yourself clearly. Think about it from their perspective: Who would you rather admit to your school? Someone who sounds like everyone else, or someone who really stands out as a unique individual? I think the choice would be clear."

—*Casey Bi*

Anjali Salooja

Hometown: Providence, RI (urban)

High School: Public college prep school, about 300 students in graduating class

GPA: 99.76 (on a 100-point scale)

SAT: 720 Math, 780 Verbal

Extracurriculars: Varsity soccer and volleyball, editor of the school newspaper, Mock Trial, Science Olympiad, student government.

Summer Activities: Studied abroad at Oxford, worked as a counselor at a Providence day camp.

Awards: Wellesley Book Award, National Merit Scholar.

Family Background and Education: Both of Anjali's parents grew up in India, immigrating the year she was born. They are both engineers and her father has a Ph.D.

Nationality/Ethnicity: Indian-American

College Acceptances: Harvard, Vassar, Georgetown, Brown, Boston University, Wesleyan
College Rejections: Yale, Columbia (wait-listed)

After growing up in a household that placed a high priority on education, it was no surprise that when Anjali Salooja got to high school, she began to set her sights on the Ivy League schools. However, she wasn't the kind of kid who strategically took AP courses to boost her GPA or joined superfluous clubs to give the appearance of an eclectic personality. Instead, she worked hard in her classes, committed herself to a few extracurricular activities, and tried to enjoy her high school years. By the time college application time came around, she had an impressive résumé but no real focus. Well aware that schools like Harvard could have their pick of applicants, she tried to make her application reflect her all-around success.

High School

At her college prep high school in Providence, Rhode Island, Anjali was the quintessential well-rounded student. She led the varsity soccer and volleyball teams, served as editor of the school newspaper, and participated in myriad other activities such as Mock Trial and student government. She also excelled academically and ultimately earned the honor of being her class's valedictorian. Looking back, Anjali admits, "I felt a lot of pressure to do everything and to do well. I didn't really understand that I would be a lot healthier and a lot more relaxed if I were doing fewer things and doing them well." At the same time, she does feel like her manic schedule did help her get in. "I think it was all worth it in the end."

The Application and Essay

Just as she was preparing to apply to colleges, Anjali suffered a shock: It appeared as though being well-rounded was no longer desirable. She says that her high school guidance counselor informed them about "how there was a shift in focus from the well-rounded student to the student with a passion in something." Anjali got really nervous at this, saying, "That just wasn't how I approached my high school career, because I didn't have a pronounced interest in only one area." With this in mind, Anjali put together her applications in a way that made being well-rounded a strength. "I ended up playing up the fact that I had been dedicated to all my activities from the very beginning and that through hard work I had gained greater responsibility in these areas." She emphasized the well-rounded aspect, she says, "because that was all I had."

Anjali estimates that she went through four or five essays before hitting upon the right topic. One failed essay, heavily pushed on her by her English teacher, was a creative piece in the form of a poem. Anjali remembers, "She wanted me to do it in the style that every line would end with 'I am.'" She pauses, then adds, "It was a terrible idea." Finally, she decided to write about an unsettling incident that happened while she was at a program at Oxford the summer before her senior year. The group was at the Museum of Modern Art, looking at a photography exhibit on poverty in developing countries. The subjects were primarily children. "I overheard a student who was in the same program I was say how surprised he was that the museum would display photographs of poor minority children as though it were art." This profoundly disturbed Anjali, and she used her essay as a way of working through her disgust. "I just wrote about how paradoxical I thought it was to be in a place that had such history, such an academic tradition, and at the same time to hear one of the most ignorant things that someone has ever said in my presence." Her Spanish teacher, an all-around academic and linguist, helped her edit the essay, and Anjali admits that it underwent at least seven, possibly up to eleven, drafts.

Contacts and Connections

Anjali says, "I didn't know anyone who was involved with Harvard or went to Harvard and definitely lamented that fact all throughout my senior year of high school." However, the regional admissions officer did call Anjali to have an interview with her in addition to her alumni interview. Anjali says that experience was invaluable. "I really felt as though we had a great conversation and that she would have pulled for me had she the opportunity."

At Harvard

Although Anjali claims to have left her well-rounded days behind, she still manages to participate in many diverse areas of the college. As president of *Current*, a national newsmagazine, she is in charge of students from multiple colleges as well as a large Harvard staff. Anjali has also written for other publications, such as *The Advocate*, and recently joined the South Asian Association and danced in their annual showcase. She has also spent the last three years sailing for Harvard's varsity sailing team.

She is a social studies concentrator with a focus on international relations. In summer 2005, she traveled to India in order to research her thesis on women's involvement in the textile industry in developing countries and its effects on traditional gender roles.

The Bottom Line

Anjali emphasizes how important it is to "play the game." She didn't try to make herself into something she wasn't, but she did make her best qualities clear. "You have to come off as though you have more of a vision of yourself and where you want to be than you necessarily do."

—*Mollie H. Chen*

William "Brad" Wainright

Hometown: Norwich, Connecticut (suburban)
High school: Public school, 2,200 students in graduating class
GPA: 4.5
SAT: 800 Math, 750 Verbal

Extracurriculars: Captain of varsity golf team, National Honor Society, math club, debate club, science club, Project Outreach Service club, chemistry lab assistant.

Summer Activities: Attended the Stanford University Math Camp where he studied number theory; attended the National Youth Leadership Forum on Medicine.

Awards: All-State and All-Conference for golf, AP National Scholar, National Merit Scholar, High Honors in the Chemistry Olympiad, high school valedictorian.

Family Background and Education: His father is a physician, and his mother is a speech pathologist.

Nationality/Ethnicity: White

College Acceptances: Harvard, MIT, Duke, Dartmouth, Johns Hopkins, University of Michigan

College Rejections: None

When William "Brad" Wainright started his early action application process during the fall of his senior year, he already had a strong standardized test résumé, with high scores on the regular SATs and eight SAT subject tests. He also had a solid background in science, having earned high honors on the U.S. Chemistry Olympiad and taken most of the AP classes at his school. One of his greatest advantages was that he had a well-rounded application. In addition to school work and science extracurriculars, Brad played on the varsity golf team and had already earned All-State honors. However, he worried that he did not have any major national activities that would really stand out on his résumé.

High School

In high school, "I took all the AP classes, eleven of them," he says. "I enjoyed chemistry, physics, biology, and calculus BC. U.S. history was all right." He took the AP exams as well and earned the "AP National Scholar" distinction from the College Board. His extracurricular activities included participation in the National Honor Society, the debate team, and the math club. "I was some type of league high scorer for a couple of years in math," he remembers.

His passion, though, was chemistry. Brad worked for his AP Chemistry teacher in the school lab. He also entered the U.S. Chemistry Olympiad, which is comprised of a series of school-level tests and then the national-level test. Brad scored high honors on the national test. Outside of academics, he played on the varsity golf team. He was team captain his senior year, finished third at the Eastern Connecticut Conference Tournament, and was named All-State his junior year. In retrospect, he believes that his All-State ranking in golf and his AP National Scholar award were his most significant accomplishments.

The Application and Essay

When he filled out his application for Harvard, Brad made sure to list all of his activities. "I didn't just use the slots they gave you," he says. "I attached a sheet to make sure I said everything." The strong points that he emphasized on the application were his golf involvement, his lab help, and his performance on the Olympiad test. He also credits his AP Chemistry teacher for writing him a great recommendation, which was spurred by Brad's exceptional performance on the Chemistry Olympiad national test. Brad also got a recommendation from his AP Economics teacher, who had attended Harvard. He feels that these strong letters helped significantly. Brad summarizes his philosophy of what is important: "Focus on academics and don't worry too much about activities."

Brad wrote his essay on golf, which was an idea that came naturally to him. "I've played golf for fifteen years and played golf all the time in high school," he says. Brad wanted to avoid just harping on his achievements in the sport. "I tried to write it to show I had fun playing golf instead of trying to impress someone with my accomplishment," he remarks. His essay focused on the times that he played golf with his friends, and also described the kindness of his coach, who would schedule events on a variety of courses for the students' benefit. On his second supplementary essay, Brad focused on the knowledge he gleaned and the experiences he had at two summer camps. He attended the National Youth Leadership Forum on Medicine the summer before senior year and Stanford University math camp the year before that. He worked efficiently on the essays and did not dwell too long on them. "No one edited them or read them," he recalls, "and I wrote them one day and edited them another."

Contacts and Connections

Brad's previous contacts with Harvard were few, and he did not benefit from any legacy advantages. When he was a junior, he attended an informational meeting hosted by the Harvard Club of Connecticut and spoke to several of the representatives there. The meeting included an admissions officer from the university as well as four alumni who discussed the application process. The alumni interviewer was an attorney from his town, and Brad kept in touch with him. He also took a tour of the campus one summer, but did not meet with any admissions officers or any university officials.

At Harvard

Now that he is at Harvard, Brad spends most of his time going to class and studying for his pre-med courses. He is a biology concentrator, and he conducted summer research at a lab at Yale University the summer after his freshman year. When he has spare time, he plays in intramural sports, and he is a member of the Pre-Med Society and the outing club. Asked what he enjoys about Harvard, Brad replies, "It's nice to be around so many smart kids. If you have any questions about class, then there's always someone who knows the answer."

The Bottom Line

Brad recommends that possible applicants work hard to earn high test scores and grades and that they only participate in activities that they enjoy instead of joining clubs solely for their résumé. For those prospective applicants who have a strong interest in science, Brad suggests that they try to take the three national Olympiad tests in chemistry, physics, and mathematics, and also enroll in all the AP science and math classes offered by their school. For those who lean more toward athletics, Brad says that they should emphasize on their application how much time they spend practicing during the off-season, which will show their dedication and large time commitment. He suggests that golfers especially should play in junior tournaments throughout the year for tournament experience.

—*David Zhou*

Strategy 4: Lead the Pack

In today's world of college admissions, academic excellence alone doesn't cut it. Colleges seek out leaders, applicants who have a record of peer leadership and civic engagement. Leadership really counts, and it's not just for your résumé. Colleges understand that it's through leadership that young adults learn to grapple with real world issues and gain interpersonal skills while they're at it. Many college students spend more time on their extracurricular activities than their academics, so it's no wonder that leadership experience weighs so heavily in admissions decisions.

Leadership takes many different forms. Some students choose to take up roles in a great variety of activities; others pursue top posts in only a few groups. Many lead activities beyond the school paper and debate team, even working with religious groups or for local politicians. Dahm Choi sat on various school councils and was the executive assistant to is mayor in Irving, California, while James Sietstra spent part of high school working for a "Get out the Vote" campaign. Amelia Kimball was a peer educator and community leader in her native New Hampshire, and Carmelo C. Tringali took a significant part in no fewer than nine extracurricular activities at his public high school. As these applicants demonstrate, there are innumerable opportunities for leadership within a school as well as in communities or local organizations.

Ask yourself a few questions to see if you could portray yourself as a leader on your college applications. Do you stand out as a leader among your peers? Was the bulk of your time in high school spent arranging meetings, juggling tasks, and overseeing projects? Do you deal well with people? Do you shine when you are in charge? Do you relish overseeing a project from start to finish, and grappling with planning and staff? If you demonstrate these qualities, it might not matter if you have perfect grades. It's your charisma that you should focus on, and you must demonstrate that in every aspect of the college admissions process.

In order to communicate your qualities on your application rather than just listing your positions in the space allotted, consider the following tips:

- Be sure to get a recommendation from somebody who has helped you hone your leadership skills or who has advised activities in which you held leadership positions.
- Be prepared to discuss difficult issues or situations that have confronted you as a leader. Your ability to grapple with real-world concerns will demonstrate maturity and skill.
- Emphasize your leadership strategies, public-speaking abilities, and interpersonal skills in your college essays.

Dahm Choi

Hometown: Irvine, CA (suburban)
High School: Public school, 600 students in graduating class
GPA: 4.0
SAT: 740 Math, 770 Verbal
Extracurriculars: Freshman class council, sophomore class vice president, associated student body representative, student member of Board of Education of Irvine Unified School District, student representative to Parent-Teacher Association Board, Orange County School-to-Work Program, School Site Council, Principal's Council, associated student body president; executive assistant to the mayor.
Summer Activities: Travel, reading, city council work.
Awards: *Los Angeles Times* Generation Next Feature Student, National Merit Finalist, AP Scholar, Korean Heritage Foundation Scholarship.
Family Background and Education: Dahm was born in South Korea but flew over to the United States after his parents had settled in the coun-

try for about a year. His mother did odd jobs, and both parents worked for a Korean-American newspaper. His parents moved to Pennsylvania, where two local families served as mentors and introduced Dahm to libraries.

Nationality/Ethnicity: Korean-American
College Acceptances: Harvard (early admission), Brown, Stanford, UC Berkeley, UCLA, Claremont-McKenna, Pomona, Stanford
College Rejections: None

Reading was the most important thing to Dahm as a child. He grew up without video games or cable and instead spent a lot of time at the local library and Barnes & Noble. A large part of his academic interest comes from growing up in an environment where most parents were professionals or academics. Dahm grew up in a tough neighborhood in North Philadelphia but was fortunate to attend one of his parents' friends' schools on scholarship from an anonymous donor. In fifth grade he moved to UC Irvine so his father could complete his dissertation.

High School
In high school, Dahm was relatively reserved and not particularly involved in student activities. He attended a highly competitive large public high school of 2,400 students. In tenth grade, he became very involved in student government and community leadership. He stresses being raised in a very intellectually nourishing environment. Dahm's two themes of high school were his attempt to learn about the world beyond high school, and his student leadership and activism.

During Dahm's junior year, the school district faced a crisis and funding was a big issue. Dahm led the effort for the board of education to increase taxes for local education. Though he received a lot of media attention, the effort failed. He was very politically involved in the community and worked in the mayor's office with his mentor, Mayor Larry Agran, a Harvard Law School alum who encouraged him to apply to Harvard throughout high school.

The Application and Essay

Dahm's application highlighted his exceptional record of community service. He stressed his dedication to education and to furthering the cause of the public schools in his community through working on civic projects and student leadership. He also emphasized his strong ability to work with adults. Dahm stressed what he had achieved in student government and in municipal politics. He felt his local activism was particularly noteworthy as this work was accessible to all and especially relevant to his fellow students.

The first line of Dahm's college essay was "We lost." He wrote the essay as a study of his thought process looking back from senior year on a very busy junior year. He wrote about his failure to raise the local taxes for education during a financial crisis and how important it had been for him to have committed himself to the extracurricular world, particularly through civic commitments and civic leadership. He described how he found these activities richly rewarding, as they brought him personal maturation as well as intellectual development and increased his curiosity for the world around him. This essay was complemented well by recommendations from Mayor Agran and the principal of his high school.

Contacts and Connections

Dahm's link to Harvard was Mayor Agran, a member of the Harvard Law School class of 1969. Agran wrote recommendations for two other students he had worked with in Dahm's class and all three were accepted to Harvard. Dahm initially earned his position as an executive assistant to the mayor by writing a letter expressing his interest on the back of a campaign solicitation reply card that was mailed to his house, and he soon began working on the future mayor's campaign. "Larry took on the role of mentor with great commitment and generosity. Strong-willed, intelligent, and dedicated, Larry was a model of personal drive, an example of thoroughness for a young person caught up in the din of high school."

At Harvard

Dahm studied history at Harvard and recently completed his senior thesis on the history of education. During his Harvard experience he has focused primarily on intellectual growth, the central theme of his application process. In the future, Dahm is interested in following his father and becoming an academic.

The Bottom Line

Of the admissions process, Dahm says, "I attended a highly competitive public high school where, admittedly, those of us in my graduating class accepted to Harvard did not earn the highest marks, take the most advanced courses, demonstrate the greatest potential in the classroom." However, Dahm says that those who were admitted had incessantly challenged each other, sustaining a curiosity for the world that, however naïve, manifested itself in daily talk about the news, political discussions, overzealous chatter about the future, shared reading lists, and friendships with everyone's parents. "We didn't have the best scores in our class, but we were the most well read."

—Erica K. Jalli

Amelia Kimball

Hometown: Sandwich, NH (rural)
High School: Private boarding school, about 340 students in graduating class
GPA: 3.9
SAT: 620 Math, 710 Verbal
Extracurriculars: Peer educator, peer mediator, peer leader, choir, volleyball, track.
Summer Activities: Counselor at a day camp; architecture and introduction to medical sciences classes at Oxford for a month, through the Oxbridge program; employment in a pizzeria.

Awards: Harvard Book Prize.
Family Background and Education: Amelia's mother attended Harvard and Boston University for graduate school, before becoming a title abstractor. Her father, now a logger, went to MIT. Her sister recently graduated from McGill University.
Nationality/Ethnicity: White
College Acceptances: Harvard, Brown, Georgetown, McGill (Canada), Washington University
College Rejections: Yale, Tufts

Despite growing up in what she describes as "the middle of nowhere" (rural New Hampshire), Amelia Kimball seems to have made the most of her opportunities. After landing herself a spot at a nearby resource-filled boarding school, Amelia immediately began to show an interest in helping those around her. After two summers spent cultivating her leadership skills as a junior camp counselor, Amelia was ready to put these skills to use, providing guidance and support for her fellow students. Amelia remained well-rounded, however, always playing a sport and singing in the chorus. "I did not have one activity I was amazing at, but I did stay busy with activities that I really cared about," Amelia says humbly.

High School
Once Amelia became involved in leadership, she followed through with vigor, working as a peer educator and mediator her junior year and a leader her senior year. At the same time she enjoyed singing in the chorus and playing on the volleyball and track teams, which she did for all four years. All of this activity contributed to Amelia's general image of being an involved member of her community.

The Application and Essay
Amelia was not overly anxious or competitive about the college application process. "I don't feel like I had a strategy," she says. "I tried to

highlight my student leadership roles while remaining completely frank and honest." She did not strive to tell the admissions officers what they wanted to hear. For example, despite the pervasive notion that community service experience is an essential credential on a college application, Amelia didn't bother mentioning her experiences, since they were scattered and inconsistent.

Amelia explains her personal essay as being about "race relations and the implication of being white in today's society—how it is important to have the majority working for the minorities as well as having minorities work for their own rights. . . . The idea evolved out of a diversity workshop I was involved in at my school," Amelia says. "I didn't start it ahead of time like other people; I probably started a month before the application was due.

"I didn't want too many people to read my essay because I wanted to make sure that it was my own thoughts, words, and style," Amelia reveals. She amends that, however, by adding that she actually did have her college counselor and English teachers read it: "I didn't have anyone who knew me that well [read it], it's kind of a private thing, so it was weird. . . . The goal of my essay was simple: to give the admissions committee an idea of who I am and how I think. I think that was a strength."

Contacts and Connections

Amelia went on a tour of Harvard and had an alumni interview. She never followed up with her interviewer, though. "I don't remember my interviewer's name or where he was from, even," Amelia admits. She made no special contact with anyone at Harvard, but her mother did go to Harvard as an undergraduate.

At Harvard

Amelia has been very active in community service: tutoring kids, working as an assistant at an after-school program, and participating in Crimson Crooners, an a cappella group that goes to nursing homes and hospitals, and "Pets as Therapy," a group that takes dogs to nursing homes. She is currently in charge of props, costumes, and set design for the freshman musical.

The Bottom Line

Throughout high school, Amelia proved herself to be a leader and not a conformist. Thus it is fitting that she did not succumb to the college application competitiveness and self-packaging that occurs so frequently these days. "The best advice that I can give is that applications are much more impressive if they are filled with activities you are passionate about, not just fillers," professes Amelia. "Ideas which interest you and aren't just what you think admissions wants to hear."

—*Nina L. Vizcarrondo*

James Sietstra

Hometown: Sioux Falls, SD (urban/suburban)
High School: Public school, 400 students in graduating class
GPA: 4.00 (unweighted)
SAT: 730 Math, 760 Verbal
Extracurriculars: Varsity policy debate captain, varsity foreign extemporaneous speaking, Student Congress representative, founder and director of Immigrant New Student Technology and Education Program (IN STEP), National Honor Society vice president, AP Physics teaching assistant, campaign worker for South Dakota senate race, French club treasurer, junior varsity tennis, church volunteer work, computer tutor for Sudanese adults and elderly, Boys State secretary of state, Straight Forward Youth Leadership Board (city), Rotarian.
Summer Activities: Intern for Morgan Stanley Investment Banking Division for senior vice president in San Francisco, policy debate camps, anti–video lottery campaign worker, South Dakota Youth Leadership Conference; South Dakota Governor's Camp; summer school (at his high school).
Awards: City Youth Volunteer of the Year Award, national qualifier for varsity policy debate and foreign extemporaneous speaking, National

Merit Scholar semifinalist student of the month, AP scholar, scholar-athlete award, poem published by *Sojourner* literary magazine, outstanding speaker award at Governor's Camp.

Family Background and Education: His mother went to Augustana College in Sioux Falls and received a master's degree from North American Baptist Seminary. His father went to Pacific University in Oregon and received a doctor-of-optometry degree from Pacific University's College of Optometry. His sister graduated from Harvard College.

Nationality/Ethnicity: White

College Acceptances: Harvard (early action), Yale

College Rejections: None

James says that he was concerned that his status as a geographical "outsider" might make it difficult to get into Ivy League schools like Harvard. He is from the only city on the prairies of South Dakota—Sioux Falls. The top student in his class and an active participant in his school and in his community, he was a well-rounded applicant. He sees as the greatest strengths of his application his accomplishments in policy debate and his role in founding a student-tutoring program for immigrants. James says that his program, IN STEP, originated from his close friendship with two Dinka Sudanese refugees. The initiative was successfully replicated at the city's other two public high schools, and James received the city's Youth Volunteer of the Year Award for his work.

High School

Gregarious and social, James laughs when he shares what he heard over and over in the spring of his senior year: "How did *you* get into Harvard?" In the wide variety of activities James participated, he was known as a capable and extremely personable leader. He genuinely likes people and personal interactions. But he is also determined to succeed in whatever he does, often spending twelve-hour days at high school and then coming home to study or tutor his Sudanese friends several more hours at night.

James was heavily involved in his church and his community, following in the steps of his mother, who is the pastor of a progressive church that actively pursues social justice. Also, James's interest in politics runs deep. One of his essays recalls the 2002 Senate elections, during which he and other volunteers worked to get out the vote in Native American reservation communities on the other side of the state. Record numbers of reservation voters turned out to the polls that year, and his candidate ended up winning by only a few hundred votes.

The Application and Essay

James put a tremendous amount of time and effort into perfecting his application to Harvard. "I approached the application knowing that I wanted to emphasize the strongest parts of my résumé," he notes. He made sure to include all of his high school accomplishments, using every opportunity available on the form to let the admissions officers know what he had been doing during those four years. He listed nearly two dozen extracurricular activities and submitted three essays. James took care to highlight his debate accomplishments as well as his work at IN STEP. "I wouldn't let myself be limited by the space provided," he says proudly. "I used several supplemental pages so I didn't have to leave anything out."

James speaks especially fondly of his three essays, which he calls "one of the strongest parts of my application." He seized the chance to let the admissions officers reading his application glimpse the person standing behind the grades and lists of activities. For that reason, James spent an extraordinary amount of time refining his essays. "I approached the essays as an opportunity to connect with my readers and give them an idea about who I really was," he says.

The first of James's essays focused on his experiences at Boys State, an educational government program run by the American Legion. In his bid for governor, the top position in the program, James was suddenly taken out of the running on a technicality. "My political plans were foiled," he wrote. But James was not ready to walk away just yet. "I knew I couldn't let this much political capital go to waste," he wrote. Although he could not serve as governor himself, James set out to throw his weight behind the person he deemed best qualified: "I reviewed my party's candidates and made the call. Drew Peterson. He wasn't very vocal, but he was a tall, strong farm kid with a big wide smile." James headed up the support structure for Drew, who went on to win the governorship. In his essay, James discussed the "powerful lesson in politics" that his experience at Boys State taught him. "I took life's lemons and made lemonade," he wrote. "In the process, I discovered that you can always find another way to succeed, and that empowering others can give you as great a sense of accomplishment as winning yourself."

In his second essay, James stayed with the theme of helping others—this time, a small group of Sudanese boys in the IN STEP program. Finally, in his personal statement, James described his exhausting work to get out the vote in Native American reservation communities. He expressed the emotions he felt when he learned that his candidate had won reelection: "For the first time in my life, I understand why political activism is important. And I understand that I want to be in places where I can make a difference, like the 2002 election in South Dakota."

Contacts and Connections

James had few connections or contacts at Harvard. His sister graduated from Harvard in 1998, but he does not think that connection played a role in the admissions process. He pursued several other routes to let the admissions office know about his interest in coming to Harvard.

James feels his Harvard interview was one of the weak spots on his application. "I had an interview during a visit to Cambridge that, at the time, I thought went really badly," he says. "I walked out of the admissions building, and I think my exact words to my sister were, 'Looks like I'm going to Yale.'"

James had the opportunity to meet his admissions officer several times when she visited South Dakota. He thought that their meetings went well. "I'm a pretty social guy, so I grabbed all the opportunities I could to meet with admissions officers and interviewers in person," he recalls. James also met with the heavyweight men's crew coach when he was in Cambridge to ask about the program.

At Harvard

Most of James's time in college is spent working in class or rowing on the river for the freshman heavyweight crew team. "Rowing takes up a lot of my time—so much that it's hard to squeeze in many other activities," he observes. But through rowing, James says, "I've met a lot of genuinely good guys. It's been a great activity." James also attends talks at the Institute of Politics. He is considering attending law school or business school, or even both. "I'm really interested in a job that allows me the opportunity to lead," he remarks.

The Bottom Line

James's advice to potential Harvard applicants centers on persistence. "Never ignore the potential of a plan B," he affirms. "Like everyone, I've had a number of failures and bumps in the road. And what I've discovered is that failing isn't as bad as we sometimes think it is. Sometimes failing provides us with an opportunity to explore the value of an alternative course—a plan B. . . . Success is rooted in seeing opportunity when others see defeat."

—*Daniel J. T. Schuker*

Carmelo C. Tringali

Hometown: Monterey, CA (suburban)
High School: Public school, 310 students in graduating class

GPA: 4.2 (weighted)

SAT: 780 Math, 640 Verbal

Extracurriculars: Junior class assistant advisor, associated student body president of Monterey High School, team captain of Monterey High School Mock Trial team, student tutor, Key Club (junior community-service club of Kiwanis) member, Spanish club member, Monterey Peninsula Unified School District Strategic Planning Team member, student board member on the Monterey Peninsula Unified School District Board of Education.

Summer Activities: California American Legion Boys State delegate, Royal Rotary Youth and Leadership Camp attendant, youth ministry for local Catholic church, Kairos Youth Ministry attendant.

Awards: National Honor Society, Outstanding Defense Attorney for Mock Trial.

Family Background and Education: Carmelo comes from a "comfortable" background, although neither of his parents graduated from college.

Nationality/Ethnicity: Italian-American

College Acceptances: Harvard, UC Davis, UC Berkeley, UCLA, UC San Diego, Georgetown

College Rejections: Yale, Stanford

Carmelo C. Tringali from Monterey, California, is a natural-born leader with ambitions in politics and a slight addiction to poker. Carmelo noticed his desire to lead and get involved with local politics early on and was thus able to pursue his interests in these areas starting in high school.

High School

In his four years, Carmelo participated in a laundry list of extracurricular activities that in some way showed the extent of his leadership skills. "My résumé was something I had been working on for two years. A portion of everything I had done was geared toward my résumé, though there were some things that I was genuinely interested in," he says. Among these activities, the most prominent were president of his school, captain of the Mock Trial team, and executive member of the Spanish club. Outside of school, Carmelo was also involved in politics as a student board member of the Monterey Peninsula Unified School District Board of Education. He was also a member of the high school branch of Kiwanis, a participant in the Rotary leadership camp, and a delegate to the California Boys State, an elite group of student leaders in his state. However, Carmelo does note that his application did lack consistency, as most of his activities had accumulated in junior and senior year. In fact, he had not participated in any one activity for all four years of high school.

The Application and Essay

When it came time to apply, Carmelo decided that he wanted to convey his leadership skills and political interests and thus molded his Harvard application in such a way as to reflect this. Of all the pieces, Carmelo decided to focus the most on his essay. His main essay was about his drive to accomplish "big things" at Harvard since he was the first member of his family to go to college. "I didn't want [the essay] to be common and I didn't want to write an essay that didn't say something about my character," he says. The idea for the essay sprang from an essay brainstorming session at a summer college preparatory camp that Carmelo attended during the summer after his junior year. With the editorial help of his camp counselors, eight drafts, and twenty to twenty-four hours later, Carmelo had completed his first college essay. The final version began with an introduction about his family and their fish business and his experiences performing manual labor while working for the business. He subsequently proceeded to write about his great sense of the meaning of hard work and his appreciation for the sacrifices his family has made to send him to college. Carmelo concluded by communicating his desire to return and contribute to his family's business with his education.

Carmelo also included a second essay in his application that he had adapted from an essay that he had used in his application to Georgetown. In the essay, Carmelo expanded on how he would take advantage of his time at Harvard. The opening paragraph placed the reader in a scene from Carmelo's Mock Trial experience, tricking the reader to believe they were reading about a law case. He later went on to talk about his passion for the legal process and government, and how the two were consistent with his desire to attend Harvard. In the end, Carmelo was sure to pitch himself as what he calls a "politics person" and to emphasize how Harvard and Boston would be a great catalyst to his ultimate hopes of becoming an attorney and politician. On this essay, Carmelo used two English teachers to edit his writing, leading to five drafts of the essay.

Contacts and Connections

Although Carmelo did not have a personal connection in the university nor any alumni in his family, he did have two supplemental letters of recommendation from influential figures. One was from a federal judge who had been a family friend and a second was from Leon Panetta, White House chief of staff during the Clinton administration and also a friend of Carmelo's family.

At Harvard

Since arriving at Harvard, Carmelo has participated as a coxswain for the freshman heavyweight crew team and joined a fraternity. As for his concentration, Carmelo has decided to stick with his original intentions and concentrate in government.

The Bottom Line

In the end, Carmelo's extensive leadership experience, excellent academic record, and supplemental letters of recommendation helped him stand out in the large crowd of Harvard applicants. Carmelo advises, however, that such letters only be used if there's a real, personal connection between the applicant and the recommender.

—*Alexander H. Greeley*

Strategy 5: Beat the Odds

Students who attend New England prep schools or private schools in New York City aren't the only ones who can attend competitive colleges. And certainly not everyone at Harvard comes from these elite institutions, either. Over half the student body comes from public schools. And those who came from private schools don't always have the typical profile: Many received special scholarships to attend these schools. Just because you don't fit the profile of a typical applicant doesn't mean that you don't have a great shot at getting into an elite school. In fact, in many cases, coming from an unusual place or possessing a unique background can improve your chances of admission, so don't shy away from discussing your roots—admissions officers want a diverse set of interesting, successful people who have taken risks and beaten the odds.

The key to the success strategy of "beating the odds" is not letting individual barriers prevent you from achieving success. For these students, success is all about taking risks, not being afraid to explore the unknown, and rising to the challenges as they are presented. These students are all "self-starters." For instance, Kwame Larbi Osseo-Asare, whose parents were born in Ghana, didn't let his immigrant background stop him from exploring areas completely foreign to an immigrant family in Queens—like Philips Exeter Academy. Brendan Corcoran is another example of an applicant who rose to the challenge that his parents gave him: constant moving and subsequent readjustment. His father, a colonel in the U.S. Air Force, moved the family from state to state or, more often, from country to country. Making the best out of his situation, Brendan fashioned a skill out of the lifestyle: He became an expert on global relations, thriving in Model Congress and diplomacy-related activities.

To figure out if this strategy is right for you, think about how you have overcome hardship or unusual family circumstances and turned them into an advantage. Has a particular kind of lifestyle presented a challenge that you have transformed into a skill? Maybe you're from an immigrant family or perhaps you grew up in a country other than the United States and can bring something particularly unique to your college that others who grew up here cannot. Unique experiences are valuable assets to admissions officers. If you've had them, don't be shy: describe them, think about them, figure out how they've made you who you are and why. If you do decide to implement this strategy, consider the following tips in crafting your application:

- *Be yourself.* Illustrate who you are in relation to what you've done. And don't try to conform to expectations—it won't get you anywhere.
- *Let your unique experience shine!* If you've had a fascinating, unconventional, or unique experience growing up, talk about it.
- *Emphasize overcoming barriers and triumphing over adversity.* If you've grown up in tough circumstances but still found some success, explain that. Outline and highlight your achievements, and don't spend too much time dwelling on the obstacles themselves. Give your story a positive spin.
- *Make sure you always play to your strengths.* This is the perfect chance to puff out your chest and brag.

In conclusion, if you've beaten the odds, or are in the process of doing so, flaunt it! Admissions committees love applicants who not only have diverse backgrounds, but understand the formative effect that their diverse experiences have had upon them.

Jinna Chung

Hometown: Bensalem, PA (suburban)

High School: Public school, 635 students in graduating class

GPA: 4.0

SAT: 740 Math, 800 Verbal

Extracurriculars: Vice president and UNICEF coordinator of community service club; member of clown troupe; secretary of speech and debate team; first alto of Bucks County Music Educators' Association Choir; member of choir, madrigal choir, and jazz choir; various principal and leading roles in dramas and musicals; co-founder of the Multicultural Awareness Organization; opening attorney of the Mock Trial team; first-grade tutor in the YWCA Early Academic Intervention Program.

Summer Activities: Secretary and Korean-English translator at Family Planning in Los Angeles, cashier and stockperson at a food market, senior intern at the office of U.S. Senator Arlen Specter, costumed performer for children's parties.

Awards: National Honor Society, National Merit finalist, *Bucks County Courier Times* 2000 Citizen Scholar, Cecelia Snyder Memorial Scholarship Award, Pennsylvania Science Talent Search Junior Award, four first-place awards at regional and state competitions of the Pennsylvania Junior Academy of Science, Superintendent's Big Five Award, 2000 Presidential Classroom Scholars Program Representative, Principal's List Awards.

Family Background and Education: Her father was at one time a student on the medical track at Seoul National University and then decided to pursue his dream of becoming an artist, dropping out of college to move to the United States with his wife about twenty-five years ago. Her mother studied at but never graduated from a teacher's college in South Korea.

Nationality/Ethnicity: Korean-American

College Acceptances: Harvard, UC Berkeley, UCLA, and George Washington (honors program)

College Rejections: None

If you've never heard Jinna Chung speak, you'd never guess she was loud. Despite her short stature, Jinna describes herself as "loud, independent, and a bit stubborn, but I'd like to think of myself as being thoughtful." Jinna was the first person in her family to graduate from college. She cheerfully describes her immigrant family as "loving but pretty unstable," one that had to deal with unique financial difficulties. Jinna humbly describes herself as "one of the average, well-rounded students who was involved in a little bit of everything as opposed to truly excelling in something."

High School

When Jinna was in middle school, her family filed for bankruptcy. Jinna, along with her sister, lived with her father in Bensalem, Pennsylvania, a lower-middle-class suburb near Philadelphia, until Jinna was in tenth grade, when Mr. Chung could no longer financially support his daughters. The girls moved to Los Angeles to live with their mother. Briefly, Jinna attended the John Marshall High School, an extremely large Los Angeles public school. However, fed up with easy classes and lack of support from the guidance department at Marshall (which has recently improved with the addition of a special magnet program for gifted students and increased support for talented students), Jinna moved back to Bensalem. Her father had already moved from the area, so Jinna lived at a friend's house for two years, finishing up high school at Bensalem High School, a medium-size public school, where she entered its separate gifted program for "high IQ" students. Despite the gifted program, the students typically underperformed on standardized tests compared to other high school students.

Jinna's high school record represents her cultural, activist, and musical interests. Her first passion was music, as Jinna was in the madrigal choir, jazz choir, and Bucks County Music Educators' Association Choir, where she was ranked first alto, in addition to taking on various roles in musical productions and playing the violin in the school orchestra. "Back then I always said that I could make myself like any class and any subject because once you start to really learn the material, you start to enjoy it," writes Jinna, but she notes a "particularly memorable experience" in her American history class because of her teacher, who debated current issues instead of lecturing from an American history textbook.

The Application and Essay

Jinna's mother encouraged her to apply to Harvard, knowing very little about colleges outside of the Ivy League. Not to be completely influenced by her parents' wishes, Jinna visited Harvard with a good friend during junior year and instantly fell in love with the campus and Harvard Square. Being able to picture herself in such an environment, Jinna resolved to apply. While she spent a lot of time thinking about and planning the application, she filled out all the forms the night before and on the day of the early action deadline. Emphasizing a "driven, independent spirit (despite a tumultuous family situation) and [her] passion for learning random stuff," Jinna asked her teachers in the gifted program to mention how she liked to read books on American history, existentialist philosophy, and literary criticism outside of class. Her guidance counselor mentioned the difficult family circumstances. As for herself, Jinna emphasized her "(then) obsession with novelist Ayn Rand's unique philosophy of objectivism."

The first line of Jinna's essay, "I like to touch women's underwear," highlighted her humorous (and unusual) outlook on life. Expounding upon a paisley-patterned multicolored nightgown from childhood that she rubbed when she was little in order to fall asleep, Jinna explained her family background, living situation, and her love for her mother, to whom the nightgown belonged and from whom Jinna was living apart at the time. Jinna had actually written the essay in eleventh grade as part of an exercise in writing fake application essays in her English class, and she submitted the essay without anyone else's edits. She was the first person from her school to get into Harvard in twenty-something years.

Contacts and Connections

Jinna had made a point of e-mailing two student leaders of the Harvard Objectivist Club before her application due to her interest in Ayn Rand. In addition, Jinna had also e-mailed Professor Daniel Gilbert to ask about his psychology research paper, since she had based a science project on one of his papers on language cognition, but did not request a letter of recommendation. Other than that, Jinna did not personally know anyone at Harvard. Her interviewer asked Jinna about the courses and books she enjoyed. For Jinna, "the interview confirmed how much emphasis Harvard places on an individual's intellectual life. . . . Harvard struck me as a school that is primarily concerned about the intellectual journey of a student."

At Harvard

Jinna revisited her Christian faith at Harvard and joined the Christian a cappella group Under Construction, in addition to several other organizations and attending church. She was manager of Under Construction for two years. After college, she moved to New York City with her college roommates and works as a litigation legal assistant at Sullivan & Cromwell, a corporate law firm.

The Bottom Line

Jinna would like to encourage students from poorer immigrant families, "especially those students from 'broken' homes or other relatively dysfunctional families," to apply to Harvard, despite their difficult circumstances or lack of expertise concerning the application process on their parents' part. She hopes that the recent changes as a result of the Harvard Financial Aid Initiative will encourage and attract students like Jinna to apply and attend Harvard.

—Shang Chen

Brendan Corcoran

Hometown: Mons, Belgium (suburban)

High School: Overseas American school for military families, 68 students in graduating class

GPA: 4.3

SAT: 760 Math, 770 Verbal

Extracurriculars: Model Congress, the Hague International Model United Nations, Model European Parliament, Model NATO, varsity baseball and football, National Honor Society, student body vice president.

Summer Activities: Worked as a clerk at the NATO base in Germany through the staff summer hire program.

Awards: Presidential Scholar semifinalist, United States Senate Youth Program Scholarship Fund semifinalist.

Family Background and Education: His father attended University of Massachusetts–Amherst and received a master's degree from Webster University, while his mother received a junior college associate degree from Labouré College in Boston. Brendan's aunt graduated from Harvard in 1984.

Nationality/Ethnicity: White

College Acceptances: Harvard (early action), Columbia, Brown, Tufts, Boston University, George Washington

College Rejections: None

Brendan Corcoran calls Boston "home"—but he's only lived in Beantown for one year of his life. His father's job, lieutenant colonel in the U.S. Air Force, has allowed Brendan to travel the globe. Born in Florida, he moved at the age of four to Boston; one year later the family moved to Oklahoma, where they lived for six and a half years. His father was then deployed to Europe, and so the Corcoran family moved again, this time to Germany.

High School

In Europe, the Corcorans resided near the German-Dutch border, which Brendan traversed each day to attend high school in the Netherlands. Finally, the family moved to the city of Mons, Belgium—home of the Supreme Headquarters, Allied Power Europe (SHAPE)—where Brendan finished his last two years of high school before returning to Boston to attend Harvard. In Germany and Belgium, Brendan lived on military bases and attended classes with an eclectic group of people from America, Germany, Greece, Poland, Spain, and Turkey, to name just a few countries. His graduating class in Belgium was composed of thirty-two Americans and thirty-six Europeans. Almost all of the graduates went on to attend college, though very few students ended up at an Ivy League institution. Nevertheless, this unique educational and living situation makes Brendan and his fellow students unique applicants for colleges all over the globe.

Brendan's high school encouraged college attendance, but it did not have a particularly strong college guidance program. It was definitely not a Harvard "feeder school"; the last student to attend Harvard from SHAPE had graduated three years before him. "The school wasn't especially helpful to kids applying to Harvard," he says, and absent somebody guiding him every step of the way, "I had to be pretty proactive about putting together my application." He found the Internet—and particularly Princeton Review message boards—to be good resources from which he could cull information on how to apply to college and to get a sense of how to craft his application. Brendan's family, rather than his school, played the central advisory role as he constructed his application, as evidenced by the fact that both his parents helped edit his college essay, though none of his teachers did.

The Application and Essay

Understandably, Brendan's travels and global understanding figured prominently in his college application: "I emphasized where I lived, the way I spent high school essentially in three different countries in Europe," he says. In particular, he was careful to stress his interactions with Europeans and his unique perspective on the post-9/11 global climate. He submitted a six-page résumé—"in retrospect probably too long," he says—in which he explained in detail his extracurricular activities, particularly his participation in Model Congress.

For his personal statement, Brendan wrote a reflection on his experiences on September 11, 2001 (overcoming initial hesitations to write about such a sensitive topic). He wrote of his feeling of powerlessness, living in Belgium but wishing he could be in the States to mourn alongside fellow Americans. But he also talked about more than that one day: "I used that moment to explain a lot about my life and my experiences in Europe," Brendan says.

Brendan's extracurricular activities likely reinforced his image in the admission committee's eyes as a person with a considerable amount of global understanding. For all four years of high school—both at the Allied Forces Northern Europe (AFNORTH) International School in the Netherlands and at the SHAPE American High School in Belgium—he participated in government simulation debate programs like Model Congress. These simulation programs allow students to reenact actual parliaments by debating and voting on bills that speak to contemporary political issues. In Belgium, model government was a required course, but Brendan says that when he moved from Germany to Belgium at the end of his sophomore year he had planned to continue the activity regardless of whether it was required or not. His extracurricular activity was not limited to model government. Brendan also played both football and baseball, and he took on leadership positions like student body vice president.

At Harvard

Now at Harvard, Brendan continues his high school passion by participating in the Harvard Model Congress. He also broadcasts games on the student radio station and is a member of the Oak Club. In the classroom, he is a government concentrator particularly interested in the international political economy.

The Bottom Line

Brendan suggests that if you are a person who has had a unique international experience, be sure to give that a lot of play in your application. More broadly, your unique perspective does not necessarily have to come from international experience. If you live in a melting pot neighborhood, or have lived with people who have a different culture than yourself, be sure to give this a lot of play in your application so that the admissions committee can appreciate your cross-cultural understanding. Where grades are viewed as only one part of a student's application, such experiences can give you a decided edge in the application process. Strategies to stress your international or cultural experiences include writing an essay on the topic and joining extracurricular or service activities that will allow you to immerse yourself in the culture. And remember, don't be shy to play up your accomplishments—that's exactly what the admissions committee wants you to do!

—*William C. Marra*

Biana Fay

Hometown: Andover, MA (suburban)
High School: Private school, 350 students in graduating class
GPA: 3.8
SAT: 800 Math, 770 Verbal
Extracurriculars: Director of a community service organization that taught middle-school science; math team; volunteer for renovating run-down playgrounds in poor neighborhoods; volunteer at the public library.
Summer Activities: Web design intern at a major teen magazine.
Awards: None.

Family Background and Education: Her mother is the vice president of a software engineering firm and her father is a hardware engineer.
Nationality/Ethnicity: Jewish-Moldavian
College Acceptances: Harvard (deferred, then admitted), MIT, Cornell, Rice, Duke, Tufts, Brandeis
College Rejections: Brown

Born in the Soviet Union, Biana Fay immigrated to the United States with her family at the tender age of five. She quickly mastered English while attending public schools and at the same time maintained fluency in Russian. By the time she graduated from an elite prep school, Biana knew languages beyond just Russian and English—as one of the school's top-rated computer science students, Biana had mastered C++, Java, Visual Basic, LISP, and HTML. From solving equations to designing Web sites, Biana proved that when it comes to math and science, it isn't a man's world.

High School

Biana devoted much of her time to public service activities. She volunteered at a public library, built playgrounds in rundown communities, and tutored underprivileged children in writing. Biana's most intense volunteer activity, however, was leading a science program for middle school girls. Every other weekend fifteen to thirty girls came to Biana's school where they observed and conducted science experiments. Biana was responsible for recruiting students and tutors, as well as designing lesson plans. "At the time I was a girl who was interested in science," Biana says, "and I thought it was important for younger girls not to get discouraged."

In the classroom Biana was one of her school's top-ranked math and science students. After taking calculus BC as a sophomore, she enrolled in classes beyond calculus, including linear algebra. "I knew that to go to a good college I needed to challenge myself," she says.

Challenging herself involved taking nine AP classes in a number of fields—European history, chemistry, Spanish, psychology, and physics, to name a few.

Biana performed well as a member of the math team, but it was computer science that interested her most. "I really enjoyed the logic involved in figuring out how to create algorithms and programs," she remembers. As part of the school's computer science team, Biana surprised her male counterparts with her quick ability to solve problems.

The Application and Essay

As a female who excelled at math and science, Biana knew she defied stereotypes. "The message of my application was, 'Look at this girl who is interested in science but also has other aspects to her.' That's how I wanted to sell myself," she remembers.

For her letters of recommendation, Biana chose teachers who taught her for multiple years. One was her Spanish teacher, who knew her for three years, and the other was her biology teacher, who taught her for two years. Because these teachers taught relatively small classes, Biana had had ample opportunity to interact with them. "They were the teachers I felt that I had the most personal relationship with." In addition to the two required letters of recommendation, Biana submitted a supplementary letter from a professor of computer science at Harvard. Biana took a computer science course at Harvard Summer School after her sophomore year and stood out—even when compared to her older classmates. "I was the best student in his class. That was surprising to the professor because I was a girl in high school, whereas others were college students or grad students."

Her computer science classes may have been a breeze, but writing the application essay proved to be more difficult. Biana went through seven draft essays and never felt totally satisfied. She thought they were too clichéd and predictable, particularly an early essay she wrote about overcoming obstacles. "It didn't bring out any aspects of my personality that weren't already in the application, other than to say generic things, like that I was tenacious, which I'm sure most applicants to Harvard are." After being deferred on her early action application with that essay, Biana wrote a more honest and personal essay that she submitted to the committee. It discussed her enchantment with city life and her daily commutes to downtown Boston during an internship at a teen magazine. "It discussed how, as my life progressed, I wanted to maintain a sense of wonder about the world." Throughout the process, Biana's mother assisted her with revisions.

Contacts and Connections

Several students from Biana's high school attend Harvard every year. She knew about life at Harvard through them, but does not feel any of these relationships necessarily gave her an edge in the admissions process.

At Harvard

At Harvard Biana explored interests outside of math and science, ultimately deciding on a major in economics. She was elected director of the Alternative Spring Break program, a group that organizes service trips for students across the country, and organized a food drive for soldiers in Iraq. She also pledged the Boo, a campus social organization.

The Bottom Line

Although Biana was a well-rounded candidate, she chose to highlight her abilities in math and science in her application. In doing so, she successfully countered prevailing gender stereotypes.

—*William L. Adams*

Jennifer L. Lykken

Hometown: Grand Forks, ND (small city)
High School: Public school, 330 students in graduating class
GPA: 4.0
SAT: 800 Math, 770 Verbal

Extracurriculars: Student council officer, member of the National Honor Society, member of the local youth symphony (first chair of flute section), math team member, American Legion auxiliary member, member of the junior varsity golf team.

Summer Activities: Jenny worked part-time jobs during the summer, as a supervisor at TCBY and as an office assistant at a pharmacy.

Awards: National Merit Finalist, North Dakota Academic Gold Award, delegate to the U.S. Senate Youth Program, Presidential Scholar, Robert C. Byrd scholarship, All-State Honor Band, individual North Dakota state MathCounts competition winner, qualified to take the AIME and USAMO math exams her sophomore year, Akamai Foundation Scholarship, American High School Mathematics Examination individual honor roll.

Family Background and Education: Her parents are high school graduates; her dad works for the Grand Forks Park District and her mom works as a legal secretary.

Nationality/Ethnicity: White

College Acceptances: Harvard, Princeton, Johns Hopkins (Bloomberg Scholarship), University of Nebraska–Lincoln, University of Minnesota–at Twin Cities, Kansas University

College Rejections: None

Jenny lights up a room with her presence, from her amused eyes to her light hair to her passionate and compassionate intelligence to her gentleness of demeanor; it is difficult not to be drawn to this irrepressible North Dakotan. One of four successful applicants from her entire state, Jenny has not let the experience change her. "My parents taught me the value of hard work. Both are very thorough and can always be counted on to follow through with their promises. They are well known for their trustworthiness, honesty, and hard work, and tried to impart these traits to me. We read a *lot* of books together as I was growing up and I became an avid reader as early as my preschool years. I ultimately chose Harvard because I felt that its location in Boston would be a great way for me to become introduced to life in a large city; also, being such a metropolitan area, there are a lot of cultural and social resources."

High School

While in high school, Jenny used every opportunity she could to get involved in the school and in local public life, including such diverse pursuits as the symphony, the math team, and the JV golf team. However, Jenny did more than pursue her scholastic and extracurricular interests; she also had other concerns. Starting at the age of sixteen and for the remainder of her high school career she worked two part-time jobs "for a total of about twenty hours per week during the school year."

The Application and Essay

In a school with about four hundred students for each guidance counselor, Jenny did not have any particular strategy when writing her application. Basically, she remembers, "I filled in the blanks with exactly what the form asked for." She did recognize that her experiences made her a distinctive and impressive candidate. As such, she emphasized her well-rounded slate of activities as well as her accomplishments in state and national mathematics competitions. Knowing all her activities should not be for her own benefit, Jenny's application also emphasized her instinctive beneficence toward others; her community service was mostly through her involvement in the "student council and NHS." Jenny occasionally ventured beyond the bounds of her regular organizations with such activities as chairing "a $5,000 fundraiser for the Make-a-wish Foundation."

As she put it, "I was very straightforward." In the end, however, she couldn't help but develop a theme. Reiterated throughout was the idea that, "although I was from a school and state that was not nearly as competitive or top-notch as many others, I still did my best to use every resource available, including extracurricular ones—AP courses, academic competitions and endeavors, music groups—to their full potential."

Once it was time to write the essay, Jenny enlisted one of her English teachers, who proofread it and offered a few suggestions. Mostly, however, this part of the process was just her pounding away at the impediments in the way of her road to success. "My essay was an analogy comparing high school to an amusement park. I edited the rest of it myself and sent it in on my own. I used a series of cute comparisons such as 'Life, like a rollercoaster, is much more exhilarating when I leave my eyes open.'"

Contacts and Connections

Jenny had "absolutely no affiliation with this school" before applying. She vaguely knew one junior at Harvard from her hometown, but for the most part "I learned everything I knew about Harvard from materials provided from the admissions office and my experiences here when I visited." She had no connections that were helpful in getting her into the school.

Applying to Harvard was a dramatic change for this girl from North Dakota. "I am a first-generation college student," Jenny reveals. "I was not even quite clear about what exactly 'early action' really was. I may have been one of only like two kids who took the SATs from my class." Most of her classmates, as well as most students in the Midwest, take the ACT. When it was time to do her interview, Jenny traveled to Fargo, a town about an hour away from where she lived. She met with an enthusiastic doctor and thinks that the interview "went really well, partly because I was very prepared. I had brainstormed beforehand about what questions might be asked and so my responses were thought out." All in all, the interview "went well because I had answers that represented who I was and I learned a lot about Harvard during the interview."

At Harvard

Jenny's activities at Harvard are just as varied as her high school activities. She spends much of her time as a psychology concentrator, as a psychology lab research assistant, and as a volunteer at Boston Medical Center. However, science does not run Jenny's life. She spends a lot of time with friends and is a member of the Undergraduate Council, the Seneca (a social club), and the Harvard University Flute Ensemble.

The Bottom Line

Jenny recognizes a lesson from her experience that she hopes other students from small towns will remember: "I just want to say that it *is* possible to get into a school like Harvard even without superb college resources," she says. "At my school there was only one guidance counselor for four hundred students, so the admissions process was something I handled completely by myself, aside from the letters of recommendation. You can research these schools yourself by going online and contacting students and visiting the campus."

—*Scoop A. Wasserstein*

Kwame Larbi Osseo-Asare

Hometown: Stroudsberg, PA (suburban)
High School: Private boarding school (in NH), over 300 students in graduating class
GPA: None assigned (A–B+ average)
SAT: 700 Math, 780 Verbal
Extracurriculars: Senior class president, Phillip's church proctor (one of six leaders of church community), founder of Current Events Forum, member of Afro-Latino Exonian Society, captain of the varsity basketball team, varsity soccer team, dorm proctor, dorm representative to Student Listeners Program (like a counselor).

Summer Activities: LEAD program in business at University of Virginia–at Darden, National Student Leadership Conference.

Awards: Perry Cup for exemplary student leadership and school spirit, Morehead Scholarship from the University of North Carolina.

Family Background and Education: Both of Kwame's parents are from Ghana, and after they got married, they came to Texas and later moved to Queens, New York. He describes them as a hardworking immigrant family. Kwame has two younger sisters, one of whom is at Cornell and the other at Princeton. Three of his cousins attended Harvard.

Nationality/Ethnicity: African-American

College Acceptances: Harvard, University of North Carolina (Morehead Scholarship)

College Rejections: None

Kwame's path to success began in middle school when he learned to balance academics and athletics. His parents encouraged their kids to try everything from music to community service to church involvement. "What I learned from my parents is that success is not solely about yourself and your accomplishments. They instilled within me the belief that we are all forever indebted to the hard work, perseverance, and determination of people who came before us and allowed us the opportunity to pursue our dreams." After a successful high school career at a prestigious New England boarding school, Kwame only applied to Harvard and the University of North Carolina. He received the John Motley Morehead Scholarship from the University of North Carolina, a four-year full scholarship to the school given to a few exceptional applicants who are leaders and scholars in their community. Despite this, Kwame decided he liked the learning environment at Harvard more, as it was more similar to his high school experience, and decided to enroll at Harvard.

High School

Kwame went to the Kent School for summer academic camp in middle school to experience being away from home at an early age, so the idea of boarding school for high school was less of a shock for him. He loved his high school, Phillips Exeter Academy, at first visit. He found the system of teaching there very intellectually forward and stimulating. Kwame's Exeter experience geared him toward a liberal arts education system like that of Harvard.

The Application and Essay

Kwame's application stressed his leadership and family upbringing. He wanted this application to convey that he was a self-starter who did not follow the beaten path. Thus, he highlighted how he founded organizations and redefined positions that others had held in the past. From the beginning of Kwame's freshman year, a local newspaper had chosen to track an Exeter student for four years so that people from outside the Exeter bubble could get a glimpse of the school and Kwame was chosen. Each article in the series examined a different theme, such as the immigrant work mentality, athleticism, or leadership. For his Harvard application, Kwame put the articles together in a nice package and sent them to the admissions office to distinguish his leadership and background.

Kwame chose to focus on his family's influence and household in his personal essay. He wrote that he had always considered himself a trailblazer, as he was raised to think independently and truly value education. His parents taught him to be a leader with a great deal of integrity. He faced the challenge of having fewer material things than his peers, but was raised to see beyond that and to put a great deal of weight on the importance of a good education. Places like local libraries were an outlet for him and helped him develop a love for learning. It is essentially a tribute to his parents and the values they instilled in him. Kwame's essay emphasized how his parents were the inspiration for all of his subsequent achievements.

Contacts and Connections

Each fall, Exeter brings all of the college admissions officers to campus and they choose different seniors to meet and talk to. The Harvard admissions officer for Exeter chose to meet with Kwame. She shadowed him for the day and observed his classes and activities. As this officer had the final say on Exeter applicants, she was Kwame's main connection to Harvard. Aside from the admissions counselor, Kwame had prior exposure to Harvard through his three cousins who were in the classes of 1998, 2000, and 2002.

At Harvard

At Harvard, Kwame was a co-founder of Joboozle.com, an interface that provides both college students and employers with a more personalized approach to the job internship recruiting process. He also served as treasurer and member of the board of the Black Men's Forum, where he helped raise $60,000 for the annual celebration of black women event. During his sophomore summer he was a private client intern for Merrill Lynch, and during his junior summer he worked as an intern for the investment bank UBS in their health-care group. Following commencement, he plans to return to UBS as a full-time analyst.

The Bottom Line

Kwame believes that the most important way to catch the attention of admissions officers is simply to set yourself apart. "Harvard hungers for students who are bright, motivated, intellectually curious, accomplished, and well-balanced. They search for and are attracted to students who have made concerted efforts to step out of their traditional comfort zones, because Harvard is a university that asks this of you on a daily basis. Therefore, the best way to be successful in the application process is to make sure that you highlight all of these key areas in your application essay, school/work activities, and personal interview. It is crucial that you provide unique examples from your life experience that will help differentiate you from the thousands of qualified applicants."

—*Erica K. Jalli*

Laura Lynn Rees

Hometown: Owensboro, KY (suburban)

High School: Public school (a national Blue Ribbon high school), 400 students in graduating class

GPA: 4.0

SAT: 790 Math, 730 Verbal

Extracurriculars: President of Beta club (an honor society), president and founder of the crochet club, member of the Academic Team, State Novice Debate Champion, Y2K Leadership Program.

Summer Activities: Church choir tour to the Boston area; Kentucky Governor's Scholars Program (GSP), a five-week academic camp; summer job at an inventory company.

Awards: National Merit Finalist, female Kentucky AP State Scholar, Harvard Book Award, Noon Optimist Outstanding Student Award.

Family Background and Education: Laura hails from a Southern Baptist background and her parents are Mennonites. They did not have a great deal of formal education, but they are quite religious.

Nationality/Ethnicity: White

College Acceptances: Harvard, Washington University, Centre College

College Rejections: None

Laura was home-schooled from the fifth to seventh grade. She essentially taught herself, reading a lot on her own. The rest of her education was through public school. She attended a high school where no one had been admitted to Harvard in decades.

Laura comes from a strong household with a strong faith, and she believes it gave her a great foundation for inquiry and individuality. "I have always respected my family, my religion, my community, my school, but I have also always challenged and questioned. I very quickly developed as a child a penchant for being an individual—I listened voraciously to my teachers, elders, friends, relations, but I also queried them on rationale, reason, and faith."

High School

Laura was very involved in her high school. "My major influences have been as such—family, friends, teachers, church. Yet I very easily adopted an attitude of independence: I needed to decide what I believed for myself. I gathered the blood-runs-thicker-than-water of my family, the loyalty of my friends, the knowledge of my teachers, and the faith of my church to build what I was before college, and what I am today. I have not lost any of these things, I have simply made them my own. One of my personal mantras is to try to take the best of the people who made a positive difference in my life and incorporate this into my own attitudes and actions. Gandhi once said, 'Be the change you want to see in the world.'"

The Application and Essay

Laura took the "I'm different" approach to her application. There were only six kids total admitted to Harvard from the state of Kentucky the year that Laura got in. She highlighted the fact that she had taken more AP tests than anyone else had in her school's history (over ten), and demonstrated that she was a leader who showed initiative. For instance, she had organized a book drive on her own for her school.

Laura emphasized her self-driven, self-taught approach, especially the fact that she paid her own way all along: She paid for all AP tests and did not take a dime from her parents after she matriculated at Harvard. She was always an overachiever and lone ranger who wanted to get out and explore a new environment.

Laura wrote her essay on Nancy Drew. She wanted to be Nancy growing up because she was a strong role model who loved to explore. Laura wrote about how she, like Nancy, wanted mystery and to get away. She ended her essay by musing that she was still waiting for her own mystery, but Nancy was always patient so she would be as well.

She had her essay read and edited by her English teacher. This teacher was a mentor, her sponsor for crochet club, and an unorthodox teacher who used the Socratic method. She also had a guidance counselor read it, but he did not like the topic. However, her English teacher told her to stick with what she felt strongly about.

Contacts and Connections

Laura had an unmemorable Harvard alumni interview with a lawyer in town, with whom she has not spoken since, as he was not particularly helpful with information. She had never visited Harvard before, and did not attend pre-frosh weekend when she was admitted. She first showed up for fall cleanup (dorm crew) and has loved it ever since.

At Harvard

At Harvard, Laura studied economics. She was a leader on campus as the secretary general and undersecretary for business for the International Relations Council (IRC). In addition, Laura led a Bible study group for the Asian-American Christian Fellowship. During her freshman summer, she worked for an environmental company. During other summers, she worked for the FDIC and for Senator Orin Hatch as well as doing economics research. Laura plans to work in Boston for the Boston Consulting Group following commencement and eventually plans to attend law school.

The Bottom Line

If you're looking for the magic admissions potion, Laura advises that you take an honest approach: "I don't know that it's really only one quality or one achievement or one part of your application—I believe that the school looks at the person as a whole, who they are, who they will be, who they want to be. You don't need to be the best at everything; you need to believe in what you do and you need to have a personal investment in life, whether that be through academics, extracurriculars, religious activities, or something else. Also, think about why you do the things that you do, and why you are the person that you are." And Laura recommends not getting overwhelmed, because "getting accepted to Harvard [or any other elite school] is not about knowing everything, it's about admitting that you might actually know very little about the world but are desperate to learn as much as you can."

—Erica K. Jalli

Nadiah Wan

Hometown: Kuala Lumpur, Malaysia (urban)
High School: Public school, 1,200 students total
GPA: 3.96
SAT: 780 Math, 800 Verbal
Extracurriculars: Debate team, cultural club, tennis, net ball, English tutoring.
Summer Activities: Biology research.
Awards: Bronze in the National Physics Quiz, distinction in the Australian Chemistry Quiz, participant in the Asian Student Exchange Program.
Family Background and Education: Her mother is Chinese, from a small town in Malaysia; she went to a two-year college. Her father is Malay, from a rural village in the jungle; he went to a four-year college and is a logistics manager.
Nationality/Ethnicity: Malaysian (Chinese-Malay)
College Acceptances: Harvard, Yale, Johns Hopkins, Brown, Penn State
College Rejections: MIT, University of Chicago

Nadiah Wan hails from Malaysia and boasts a mixed Chinese-Malaysian heritage. She speaks fluent Cantonese, Malay, and English and can translate from one to another with ease. Nadiah is a self-declared bookworm extraordinaire; she has always been interested in a wide range of academic topics from history to biochemistry, the latter ending up being her college major. Nadiah is always friendly and outgoing—a necessity, she explains, when you're a foreigner in a new country. Her story of applying and being accepted to American universities as an international student holds some important lessons for those hoping to follow in her footsteps.

High School

As Nadiah will tell you, an illustrious high school is not a prerequisite to attend Harvard. She was the first "Ivy" student ever to graduate from her school, not to mention one of the very few in school history who went on to attend an American university. At the small, public Malay high school she attended in Kuala Lumpur, Nadiah was an all-star student and athlete, running track and playing tennis, as well as debating and competing in national-level academic quizzes. In her modest manner, Nadiah downplays her many activities as the natural consequence of attending a small school, explaining that half the track team was also on the tennis team. Still, Nadiah was always first in line to fill any empty extracurricular niche, and most important, she enjoyed every minute of it. Throughout high school, she was involved in the Cultural Club, the prestigious Asian Student Exchange program, and her share of science competitions, receiving Bronze at the National Physics Quiz and Distinction in the Australian Chemistry Quiz.

The Application and Essay

Nadiah first seriously considered applying to Harvard to appease her father, who pressured her to apply because a family friend's son had been accepted the year before. She used to resent such comparisons, but now that she's enjoying herself at Harvard, she's let it go. All in all, only fifteen students applied to Harvard from Malaysia that year; only Nadiah was accepted.

What set her apart? Rather than emphasizing her intelligence, an overexpressed attribute shared by most Harvard applicants, Nadiah fostered a theme of "diversity" in her application. She highlighted her well-rounded skills and myriad interests and activities, but mostly she portrayed the hardships and limitations of her environment, and how she has overcome them. In a nation divided among Chinese-Malay race lines, being mixed Chinese-Malay left Nadiah out of both social and cultural groups. Hers was a complex cultural experience— neither parent spoke the native language of the other—and throughout her life she never really belonged in either Chinese or Malaysian culture, only fitting in with others who were mixed like her. Her portrayal of an emotionally and psychologically challenging atmosphere, as well as the criticism of a divided society, brought an air of maturity to her application.

In addition, Nadiah took a risk and criticized the British one-track school system that she grew up in, which limits exploration of fields outside one's career focus. Nadiah, who pursued a science track, resented being cut off from history and literature, subjects which she had always enjoyed. Taken as a whole, Nadiah's application was packaged as a poignant yet optimistic social critique from a young, promising mind that felt academically and socially stifled.

Her essay would ultimately complement the rest of her application, but Nadiah admits she was uninspired until the day before the application was due; in other words, she procrastinated. What she ended up writing was a thought piece on stray mongrels, which she posited as analogous to herself in terms of cultural identity. Her ultimate selling point was that Harvard would be a place where she'd belong. The school is known for its diversity, for uniting great minds from around the world. At Harvard, Nadiah argued, there is no norm and there is no "generic." Nadiah appealed to the admissions committee to let her join a student population that allowed free thinking, free exploration, and a diversity of cultures. While her essay didn't thrill her parents, Nadiah shrugged off their reservations and submitted it anyway.

Contacts and Connections

Coming from Malaysia, Nadiah's Harvard connections were sparse. A family friend had been accepted the year before, but beyond him she knew of no one else affiliated with the university. The first time she met a Harvard alumnus was at her interview, when she met with a seasoned academic and politician from the Harvard Club in Malaysia. Having interviewed many bright and ambitious students in his time, his questions focused not on her achievements, but on the topic of her essay: fitting in at Harvard. Noting that Nadiah was Muslim, the interviewer must have assumed that she was a religious conservative, and with true concern he asked Nadiah the memorable question: "Do you know they have sex there?" Few questions could have made the interview more awkward. Though Nadiah speaks pleasantly of her interviewer, he is a Harvard connection she doesn't think she'll be using any time in the near future.

At Harvard

Nadiah says that the stereotypes about overly conservative Muslims have died down quite a bit since she matriculated. She personally helps to dispel these notions on an everyday basis through her behavior—she really fits right in with all the other overachievers of Harvard. She's gotten involved outside the classroom, volunteering for Habitat for Humanity and participating in the Malaysian Student Association at MIT. Academically, she's a biochemistry concentrator, and you're likely to find her working long hours at a virology lab on campus. On winter weekends, she manages to find time to sneak away and go snowboarding, which is one of the main benefits of the harsh Boston winters.

The Bottom Line

Nadiah acknowledges that applying as an international student is tough, but she counsels that international applicants should emphasize the unique cultural and philosophical diversity that they could offer to the Harvard community. "Everybody who applies to Harvard will be smart," says Nadiah. "Grades and test scores are very important, but talking about them for most of your application won't set you apart. Focus on who you are, where you come from, what you can bring to Harvard, and all the achievements you have accomplished aside from academics. You have to be yourself throughout. That's what's most impressive. That's what they will look for."

—*YiDing Yu*

Strategy 6: Write the Standout Essay

Many Harvard applicants will be able to run down a litany of prizes they won and extracurriculars they headed in high school. Stellar SAT scores and grades are the norm. The personal essay, though, is your chance to distinguish yourself in the eyes of the admissions office, to be creative and to communicate something about yourself that doesn't necessarily appear on your résumé. The essay is the place to showcase your passions and to explain why something that only garnered three lines on your résumé actually signals a unique contribution you could make to Harvard.

There is no template for writing an excellent essay—in fact, almost any subject can work. Successful essays convey something about an applicant's personality and outlook on life. The applicants featured in this chapter wrote about subjects ranging from extracurricular activities to personal trials and triumphs to the way their cultural and national heritage has impacted their life. Although writing about a summer job or activity might seem boring, what's important is what you highlight. Essays in this chapter focused on the out-of-the-ordinary—the first day on the job where a student made a ton of mistakes and how she learned from that experience, or the time at a debate competition where participants rallied to change the debate organizers' policy on displaying flags. One other student here took a unique approach, penning an attack on the College Board and AP tests as monopolistic and superficial.

Although anyone can write a great essay, if you love writing and have made that a major part of your application, this is the chance to show off your talents. If you have had a unique experience—like a family or personal crisis, an unusual upbringing or cultural heritage—the essay could be a major asset for you. If you feel that something in your application is more important to you than how it looks on paper, the essay might be the place to explore and explain it. Try to focus on an experience that has been important in your development as a student or person, or on a passion that you feel explains your character.

As you prepare your admissions essay, consider the following tips:

- *Start early and revise often.* Successful applicants also asked friends and mentors to read their essays and offer suggestions.
- *Write more than one essay.* If you have the option to write a supplemental essay, consider doing so even if it is not required.
- *Don't be afraid to be creative.* Successful essays aren't always about events or activities—they might be about ideas you have or a subject that's important to you.
- *Try to stand out.* Admissions officers are looking at tons of essays; write on a unique subject or in a way that you're sure no one else will write.

Darja Djordjevic

Hometown: Chicago, IL (urban)
High School: Private "laboratory" school, about 120 students in graduating class
GPA: 4.0.
SAT: 720 Math, 750 Verbal
Extracurriculars: President of Science Olympiad team, editor-in-chief of *The Renaissance Magazine* at high school, violinist in Chicago Youth Symphony, music school, Book Initiative Committee leader, member of school's Model UN team.
Summer Activities: Toured with the Arcady Music Festival Tour on the Isterial Coastline of the Adriatic Sea as a violinist, participated in the Oxbridge International Program in Paris at the Académie de Paris, worked as research assistant at the University of Chicago microbiology lab and later in

a lab specializing in enzyme kinetics, studied Italian in Florence in the Istituto Italiano program.

Awards: American Association of Teachers of French, first regionally, fifth nationally (twelfth grade); finalist in Columbia College Chicago Young Authors Contest; Honorable Mention Award for story *Heat*; Bryn Mawr College President's Book Award; National Science Olympiad Regional Tournament, second place in Pathology/Biology, second place in Geology; Illinois State Scholar Award; French Literature Award from Académie de Paris 2002 (Oxbridge Academic Programs); University of Chicago Laboratory Schools Citizenship Award.

Family Background and Education: Father works for a furniture retail company and has a B.A. and M.A. in economics from University of Belgrade; her mother is a lecturer at the University of Chicago with a B.A. and M.A. in comparative literature and Slavic languages from the University of Belgrade.

Nationality/Ethnicity: Serbian-American

College Acceptances: Harvard, University of Chicago, MIT, Reed, Wesleyan, Columbia

College Rejections: Yale, Princeton

Darja Djordjevic is intellectually curious about both the scientific and artistic worlds. She follows her passions, whether they take her deep into a laboratory or across the Atlantic to a Parisian café. She describes herself as a well-rounded scholar who is excited at the very pursuit of knowledge and art.

High School

Darja cultivated her interests as a musician, scientist, writer, and art critic during high school. Besides being president of her school's Science Olympiad team, she played violin in the Chicago Youth Symphony, led her school's Book Initiative Committee, which brought an author of a book assigned to all students every year to speak at the school, and was editor-in-chief of *The Renaissance Magazine* during its twenty-fifth anniversary year. "I was honored to be leading the serious discussions that went into selecting twenty literary pieces out of more than 220 submissions," she says of her role in the magazine. "Artistic output of some kind and publishing the contemporary work of my generation has always been near to my heart. In fact, I read a lot of new fiction, go to see modern art quite often, and discover new music all the time. For me, this is like breathing. It is partaking in my own era and seeking to engage myself with fellow human beings."

Darja also treasures the moments she spent overseas during her summers, soaking in different cultures, particularly with the Oxbridge International Program in Paris, France. "I became best friends with someone who is now a member of [my class at Harvard], and we spent the entire day speaking French, outside of our immersion courses in French lit and art history," she says. "This friend opened my eyes to the legacy of Avant-Garde Paris, the Dadaists and Surrealists, and naturally, the bookstore culture of Paris. This historical awakening brought me unique adventures, amazing friends, and more contact with the French than I would have had otherwise."

The Application and Essay

In her college application, Darja showed her curiosity about the world and her love of all sorts of different subjects. She especially emphasized her love of learning, writing, and music. Darja also included a supplementary recommendation letter from an anthropology professor at University of Chicago she had worked with, Professor Raymond Fogelson, in addition to an essay she had written on Hamlet and poetry published in *Renaissance*.

Her common application essay was a creative piece she calls "Proustian" that was about "having two worlds—in America and Belgrade" and how these worlds "came together" after the 1999 unrest in Eastern Europe. Darja, who is Serbian-American, says this essay was "honest" and was the best thing she had ever written. "My essay was a strength of my application," she says. "I had at least six adult friends read it. I wrote about five drafts. The genesis came from being bored with the essay I had, and thinking about the effects of my bicultural upbringing, the tensions and tragedy of the Balkans that came with the '90s, as well as facing myself as a polyglot of sorts. The time period I wrote about was from seventh grade and beyond, so one's essay need not be focused on high school."

Contacts and Connections

Darja had no connections to Harvard before her acceptance. "I knew none of the professors, none of the interviewers, and none of the admissions staff before or after my April acceptance," she says. She doesn't have the most positive report of her interview either. "I felt no connection with my interviewer at Harvard in November of 2003. I had more fun at the alumni interview in Chicago, with a theologian-scholar whose area is Islam and its history," she says. When she was deferred on early action, she sent Harvard notice of new awards and writing in January, and was admitted into the regular decision pool later.

At Harvard

So far, Darja has mainly focused on cultivating her music and community service abilities. She is the assistant principal violinist in the Bach Society Orchestra and works in the community service musical group MINUHET. She is a University Health Services representative and participated in Mather House chamber music last semester. She is taking subsidized private violin lessons from the University as well, and is focused mainly on music and community service.

On applying to Harvard and looking back on her first year there, she says, "I applied to Harvard because I expected an unparalleled caliber in my fellow students and in the resources." She thinks that Harvard has ended up being a perfect place to cultivate her various pursuits. "Because I had very diverse interests and was not attached to only one study or one activity I needed a place like Harvard because it could cater to everything," she says, adding that Harvard is a good place "for people who might not know what they'll end up doing."

The Bottom Line

Darja, who believes in appreciating art for art's sake, advises applicants to have the same attitude in their applications. "Be yourself, always," she says. "Read your favorite writers or journalists during senior year to get inspired. Don't write something that doesn't move or captivate (in some way) you yourself!"

—*Katie M. Gray*

Harrison Greenbaum

Hometown: Woodmere, NY (suburban)

High School: Public school, 257 students in graduating class

GPA: 103–105 on a 100-point scale

SAT: 690 Math, 800 Verbal

Extracurriculars: Editor-in-chief of yearbook, co-editor-in-chief of school newspaper, Mathletes team captain, Web page club president, mixed-chorus president, leading player in drama club, temple volunteer.

Summer Activities: Harrison life-guarded at the beach near his home and taught swimming to children; he also attended a magic camp every year.

Awards: National Honor Roll, National Honor Roll Gold Elite, Who's Who Among American High School Students, National Merit Scholarship Commended Student, Yale Book Award, George Washington University's School of Engineering and Applied Science Medal, AP Scholar, Principal's Leadership Award, Coca-Cola Scholar Semi-Finalist, National Honor Society, Spanish Honor Society vice president, Tri-M Honor Society, All-County Chorus, Lawrence High School High Honor Roll, Federation of Jewish Men's Clubs Youth Leader of the Year.

Family Background and Education: His mother graduated from City University of New York and his father from Brooklyn College. Harrison's father is a vice president of a real-estate company and his mother is also involved in real estate.

Nationality/Ethnicity: Jewish, of Czech and German descent
College Acceptances: Harvard (early admission), SUNY Binghamton
College Rejections: Yale (wait-listed), Princeton (wait-listed)

Pick a card, any card. Write your name on it. Put it back in the deck. Harrison Greenbaum will throw the deck at the ceiling and when it falls, your card will remain stuck to the ceiling. Harrison, a professional magician since ninth grade and a member of the Society for American Magicians and the Harvard Magic Society, became interested in magic when he received his first magic set as a Hanukkah gift at the age of five. The psychology concentrator, who is also in the midst of writing a children's book, characterizes magic as "a big part of my life, and it's incredible to be at Harvard because now I get to perform in the Mystery Lounge, the longest-running magic show in Boston." Harrison's home is in suburban Long Island, fifteen minutes from the beach, with his parents and one younger sister. In the summer, he works as a lifeguard.

High School
During his senior year of high school, Harrison served as the editor-in-chief of his school's yearbook and co-editor-in-chief of the newspaper. He began both activities with staff positions in ninth grade and advanced through the editorial ranks. As a freshman, he joined the Mathletes, an interscholastic math team and became team captain as a senior. His involvement in the school's Web page club also began in ninth grade and he served as president of the club his junior and senior year; he was also the student Web master of the school's Web site. He designed and maintains his own Web site, one of the most widely read magic blogs on the Internet.

As part of the drama club, Harrison landed roles in *The Pajama Game*, was the second lead in *BIG, the Musical*, and had leading roles in *A Midsummer Night's Dream*, *A Chorus Line*, and *A Streetcar Named Desire*. He served as student director of both *A Chorus Line* and *A Streetcar Named Desire* and starred in *Damn Yankees* and *Arsenic and*

Old Lace. Harrison, who became interested in theater at a young age because his grandma took him to Broadway shows, calls himself a "Broadway baby" and says that he enjoyed playing Teddy in *Arsenic and Old Lace* because "how often do you get to be crazy in front of a hundred people every night?" As a member of his school's chorus since his sophomore year, Harrison became president of the mixed chorus, and became student advisor and vocal director of "Cabaret Night," which he founded. He soloed in Walt Disney World Magic Music Days and was a member of the select show choir.

Harrison also volunteered at his temple, performing magic for events there, in retirement homes, and for Special Olympics. As a member of the Lawrence Philharmonic, he performed for the community and captained a team for Relay for Life to raise money for breast cancer research. Outside of school, Harrison enjoys scuba-diving and is certified by the Professional Association of Diving Instructors.

The Application and Essay

Harrison shaped his application with an emphasis on his interest in magic. To enhance his application, Harrison included supplementary materials. He sent a copy of his school newspaper in which he had written the front page article and formatted a large portion of it. "I had laid out the Arts and Leisure section of that paper because it was my baby, so I was able to give the admissions committee a paper that had a good sampling of my work," says Harrison. He also included a CD of his singing and a DVD of a magic performance. "It's one thing to say you do magic," says Harrison, "it's another thing for the admissions committee to say, 'Wow, this guy really knows magic!'"

Harrison chose to write his essay about magic. He included a mentalism magic trick in the essay for the admissions staff to try. His grandma, who is an English teacher, looked at the essay for him and his parents also read it. Harrison credits an English teacher at his high school for helping him to tighten up the essay.

He also chose to write a supplemental essay, which he characterizes as much more personal. In it, he described how his quest for knowledge made him feel like a social outcast at times and how he connected to a book that felt nearly autobiographical, *Archibald Frisby*, by Michael Chesworth. He says he thinks it is important to be open and honest with the admissions staff: "If you tell them something personal," he says, "they feel they know you better."

Contacts and Connections

Although a few students from his high school had previously attended Harvard, Harrison did not have any close contacts there. He slept over in March after he was accepted, but comments, "No legacy here, I'm the first person to be in the Ivy League in my family. My father's parents were Holocaust survivors," though he says he neglected to mention that in his application. Harrison felt that his interview went well; it lasted about forty-five minutes to an hour. Harrison wrote a thank-you note to his interviewer and his interviewer called after Harrison was notified of his acceptance.

At Harvard

Harrison is in the Harvard freshman musical; he still enjoys singing and is filming a David Blaine–style TV show, highlighting street magic, called *Harvard Magic*. He is a member of the First Year Social Committee, a part of the undergraduate council. He is also a performer in a show called *Graffiti*, which he characterizes as "*Stomp* meets *Bring in 'da Noise, Bring in 'da Funk*, meets David Copperfield—an urban variety show with dancers, poets, percussionists, slam poetry, graffiti artists, and double Dutch." He is a member of Alpha Epsilon Pi, a Jewish fraternity, and is active with the Harvard financial analyst club. This year, he co-founded Disney Night, and coordinates the showing of Disney movies on Thursday nights at Stoughton, a freshman dorm.

The Bottom Line

Harrison recommends that applicants emphasize whatever it is that is unique to them. "The major important thing about an application is to emphasize the hook—you need to emphasize the thing that says 'I'm not just another one of those valedictorian people applying.' You need to drive home the thing that really makes you different from everyone else," advises Harrison.

—*Megan C. Harney*

Katherine Koopman

Hometown: Arlington, VA (urban/suburban)

High School: Science and technology magnet school, 420 students in graduating class

GPA: 3.89

SAT: 660 Math, 700 Verbal

Extracurriculars: Acted, directed, and did tech work for her high school's theater productions; acted as drama club treasurer; sat on the Council of Presidents; co-founded "Starworks Community Theater"; served as the public relations representative of the Hispanic Alliance club and later as co-president.

Summer Activities: Attended summer school in order to fulfill her school's computer science class requirement; went to the Governor's School for Spanish for a three-week immersion program run by the state; spent three weeks at the University of Chicago to take a developmental psychology course; undertook a "mentorship" through her school, for which she spent the summer before her senior year researching epilepsy at the Krasnow Institute for Advanced Study at George Mason University.

Awards: AP Scholar.

Family Background and Education: Her mother went to Georgetown and Boston College for a Ph.D. in economics and is now an economist. Her father went to University of Southern Maine and then Boston College for an economics degree; he is now the chief economist at the International Trade Commission.

Nationality/Ethnicity: Cuban-American

College Acceptances: University of Virginia (Echols Program), Washington University, UNC

College Rejections: Yale, University of Pennsylvania.

Katie Koopman's high school counselor told Katie early on in high school that "everyone has things they like; you have to *do* things that show what you like." For Katie, these "things" turned out to be neurological development, drama, and Hispanic culture; Katie spent much of her high school career cultivating her interests in these three areas. Moreover, she put the extra time and effort into her areas of interest and often sought leadership opportunities within them. Ultimately, Katie drew on the thought she put into Hispanic awareness for the personal essay of her application. Her essay on what "being Hispanic" meant to her would have been significantly different if she had not involved herself in activities that pertained to the issue.

Katie considers her high school counselor to have been a real asset to her college application process, because it was this counselor who helped her through the project and "got her started really early." However, Katie feels that she had the disadvantage of "coming from a magnet school [where] there was a lot of competition—[since] colleges don't like to accept too many kids from one school."

High School

Katie was involved in drama all four years of high school, acting in six plays, two musicals, directing three one-act plays and often moonlighting as a technician. She was even involved in the administrative side of her high school drama program, acting as treasurer of the drama club and a member of the Council of Presidents her senior year. But Katie took her interest in drama an extra creative and impressive step further when she and her friends founded "Starworks Community Theatre," a group that preformed fairy tales at nursing homes, libraries, etc. Katie says that she thinks she was perceived as a "hard worker, dedicated and passionate" by her drama peers.

Katie's mother is Cuban and Katie has always had a weakness for Cuban food, but it was not until she entered her high school (with its lack of other Hispanic students) that she was pigeon-holed as a symbol of diversity. She then began to actively explore her interest in Hispanic culture by serving as the public relations representative of the Hispanic Alliance club as a junior and co-president of the club as a senior. Katie also strived to master Spanish, taking every possible Spanish class her school offered.

The Application and Essay

Katie's approach to her application was to emphasize her main interests, in theater, neurobiology, and Hispanic culture, and to demonstrate how proactive she had been in pursuing them. Katie applied early admission to Harvard and was initially deferred.

The idea for Katie's essay arose out of fighting with her mom over whether or not she should check off "Hispanic" on her application. At first, Katie did not want to because she was worried that college admission officers would hold the same stereotypes as she did about Hispanic people, assuming she came from a poor neighborhood, etc. Thus, Katie's essay was about how "being Hispanic [was] actually a part of [her] life, albeit a confusing one," as she phrases it. Not only does she feel that writing it was a process of "self-discovery," but she also considers it to be a strength of her application. "I feel it most clearly expressed who I was and it did a much better job than any activities grid or SAT scores," she says. She wrote twelve drafts in "many different ways" and had her English teacher read it multiple times, not to mention her friends, she says, who she drove crazy by making them read nearly every draft.

Contacts and Connections

Katie looked at Harvard the summer before her junior year of high school but had no connections or contacts there, aside from students who had graduated from her high school. Of her alumni interview, she says, "I liked my interviewer a lot. . . . I wouldn't say that [we] formed a connection, but it wasn't . . . awkward." Katie didn't follow up with her interviewer, but, in retrospect, thinks that she should have.

At Harvard

In the fall, Katie sang with Kuumba, which she calls a "non-denominational gospel choir." Currently, she is in the ensemble of the freshman musical and works as a research assistant in a developmental studies psychology lab.

The Bottom Line

"The college application process is a crap shoot and you never know where you're going to get in," says Katie. So, "just be yourself on the application, because colleges use that to judge whether or not you'll do well in their environment," she advises. Katie's essay, with its honesty and thoughtfulness about such a personal and perplexing issue, is a perfect example of her "being herself" and very well may have been her key to opening the gates of Harvard Yard.

—*Nina L. Vizcarrondo*

Judith Li

Hometown: Cupertino, CA (suburban)
High School: Public school, 497 students in graduating class
GPA: 4.0
SAT: 800 Math, 800 Verbal

Extracurriculars: Editor of the school paper, concertmistress for the El Camino Youth Symphony, president of Amnesty International and Future Physicians of America.

Summer Activities: Debate camp, volunteer at a local hospital, a month-long tour in France with youth orchestra, tutoring program at Brighter Future Learning Center, SAT presentation for two Asian parent organizations, and an SAT tutoring class.

Awards: Presidential Scholar, National Merit Scholar, Governor's Scholar in Math and Science, AP Distinguished Scholar, recipient of the Tylenol Young Students Scholarship, commendations from U.S. Senators Barbara Boxer and Diane Feinstein.

Family Background and Education: Mother and father attended Taiwan University, the top university in Taiwan. Father is currently a director at a computer company in the Silicon Valley and mother is an accountant at a nonprofit that does international disaster relief.

Nationality/Ethnicity: Taiwanese-American

College Acceptances: Harvard, Stanford, MIT, Duke, University of Pennsylvania, Brown, Rice, UC Berkeley, UCLA

College Rejections: Princeton (wait-listed)

"I am a life enthusiast of unfocused talent, having gone through life mostly observing and synthesizing the experiences of others and collecting ephemeral wafts of the wayside roses," says Judith Li when asked to describe herself in fifty words or less. Judith managed to distribute her time over diverse interests and excel in all areas to become a well-rounded applicant. Like most Harvard applicants, her strength lay in her academic accomplishments. Judith also made sure to highlight and further develop her identity in her application through her extracurricular involvements, including a career with the piano that ended prematurely.

High School

Judith attended Monta Vista High School in Cupertino, California, a public high school that was essentially a magnet school. She had moved into that area, which is a predominantly Asian suburb near the San Francisco Bay Area, in sixth grade. The school population was around 2,100 with around 60 percent Asian-American students, most coming from the upper-middle-class income bracket. The environment was described as "competitive," and Judith was valedictorian of a class of 497 students. She was the editor of the school newspaper, concertmistress of the El Camino Youth Symphony for a couple of years, and also president of Amnesty International and Future Physicians of America. Her favorite classes included AP literature and AP biology, partly because the instructors for those were rather excellent. Both of Judith's parents possess strong academic backgrounds, and this no doubt created "an innate sense of pressure" on Judith. She says that her parents "never explicitly mentioned high expectations, but that does not imply that those impossible expectations were not there." Academics were definitely Judith's strength and focus, but she also pursued as many interests as she could beyond a mere superficial level. She laughs, admitting that "this, of course, led to very little sleep."

The Application and Essay

Despite losing sleep to her many involvements, Judith's myriad interests gave her "a relative ease when shaping a theme into the application," a theme which she defines as "the academic who can do other things too." In the end, academics still remained her primary focus, as Judith writes, "At the end I still relied on my academic side to craft the application. Though I had extracurricular involvements, I still think what made me stand out was the unique academic record I had in high school." Judith adds, "I sometimes wish there was one defining aspect that could be so pulling that it would forcibly wrap my life around it. There is, fortunately or unfortunately, no such thing."

Judith played an instrument. However, her promising eleven-year career as a classical pianist was terminated due to the growth of a "ganglion cyst" in her wrist early in her sophomore year. Judith had already won various competitions on a local and state scale, including a second-place finish at the U.S. Open Piano Showcase Solo in 2000. Her parents had placed her on the pre-Juilliard track, but the injury forced her to stop. This life-changing decision inspired Judith to write her parody admissions essay titled "My Ordinary Non-Tear-Jerking Life," where she complained of a lack of issues in her life, resulting in a possibly boring essay. In the crafting of this essay, Judith notes that "I then remembered the tragedy that I had convinced myself was not a tragedy; constructing the essay helped me bring out emotions I had hidden, making for a good life experience overall." Her primary proofreaders were her parents, her college counselor, and her AP English instructor, who cried upon reading the essay, despite the title. Judith avoided writing about being Asian-American out of fear of sounding cliché, but she believes that "ironically, glimpses of these struggles resurface again and again in the essay, reflecting the inescapability of these influences in the shaping of [young minds]."

Contacts and Connections

Judith, like many others who applied to Harvard, was not able to meet with anyone during the application process other than her interviewer. Judith describes her as a "young Asian-American from Connecticut (about twenty-four years old) working at eBay." Through her interviewer, whom Judith remembers as "incredibly nice and incredibly encouraging," she was able to gain confidence in the application process and not feel so much like the "little fish in a big pond."

At Harvard

Judith is currently majoring in neurobiology. She serves as a director for both the Hepatitis B Initiative and the Tzu Chi Foundation for Disaster Relief. Judith is interested in public health work, and hopes to pursue an M.D./J.D. joint degree after college.

The Bottom Line

Honesty and genuine presentation are what Judith emphasizes in applying to college. She writes that "college applications are all about 'fit.' If you 'fit' at a certain place, that will shine through." She adds that "even if you find that you don't get into the college you think you belong at, you'll find that the application process ensures you will [end up] somewhere where you will be happy."

—*Shang Chen*

Sahil Mahtani

Hometown: Jakarta, Indonesia (urban)

High School: Private school, 34 students in graduating class

GPA: No GPA system

SAT: No SAT; IB score 36

Extracurriculars: Student council president, member of the debate club, wrote and directed two plays.

Summer Activities: Not available.

Awards: Indonesian national debate champion.

Family Background and Education: Both parents attended college briefly.

Nationality/Ethnicity: Indonesian/Sindhi

College Acceptances: Harvard, Princeton, Northwestern, Middlebury University of Pennsylvania, New York University, USC

College Rejections: Oxford, Yale, UCLA

From a cosmopolitan Indonesian background, Sahil attended a very small private high school and decided to travel overseas for college. Both of his parents attended college briefly, but his grandparents did not.

High School

While in secondary school, Sahil was extremely involved in debating. He competed for his school in debate tournaments. When he wasn't competing, Sahil helped run tournaments and mentor future debaters. Sahil's dedication to debate is a sign of how important debating was to him. The other activity that took a great portion of his time in high school was student council. Through hard work and good time management, Sahil was able to become president of the student council while remaining very involved in debate. His involvement and dedication were understood by his peers, which is how he was elected president. But Sahil's passion went beyond debating and working for student council; he was also a lover of the arts. While working hard on debate and student council, he found time to write and direct two plays as well as occasionally compose music.

The Application and Essay

His application to Harvard emphasized his character traits through his participation in these activities. He wanted his application to get three major points across to its readers: his dedication to activities, his leadership skills, and what he would bring to Harvard as an international student. To emphasize his dedication, he focused on the lessons he learned through participating in debate and the considerable amount of time he spent working for the debate team. He felt that his recommendations and his positions in the student council were good ways to convey his qualities and abilities as a leader. As a final touch, he also played up his internationalism both through his extensive travel for debating as well as his experience as a minority (Sindhi) in Indonesia.

His personal essay tied together his strong qualities with a story about a policy that he and his peers considered unjust and how they resisted this policy in a respectful and justified manner. During an international debate tournament, officials refused to allow the debating teams to hang up flags in a debate against Israelis. Sahil and his fellow debaters rallied against this policy, and in the end they put up the flags of the debating teams representing each country. Sahil felt that this essay was one that unified the underlying themes of his application. Juxtaposed on the backdrop of debate, his decision to disobey when he felt a rule was wrong was a clear indication of his leadership skills, and his fight to allow students to hang their flags showed the tolerance and understanding that an international student can bring to a community. The idea came to him fairly easily, since debating was such a large part of his high school life.

His second essay focused more specifically on his internationalism, its origins, and its consequences. It described how his family felt a lack of roots due to frequent moves and his experiences as a minority in Indonesia.

Contacts and Connections

Sahil had no connections or contacts at Harvard, and he was also unable to visit, but he feels he made the right choice. "I wasn't in touch with anyone before or after I was admitted," says Sahil. Sahil also jokes that being from Indonesia, connections weren't exactly the norm.

At Harvard

Sahil Mahtani intends to study either government or economics at Harvard, and he has been enjoying himself. He still debates, but he plans to expand his extracurricular horizons by trying to join the staff at *The Harvard Crimson*.

The Bottom Line

Sahil's application had a strong focus on his activities and his abilities as a leader, but it was also very focused on his experiences as an Indonesian. Most important, it managed to connect these aspects together in a coherent fashion without seeming forced. The essay is especially important on applications like this, where the student is trying to convey nuanced character and many different values, because it allows him or her to tie together many different aspects into a coherent whole that the admissions office can relate to.

—*Nicholas A. Molina*

Sue Meng

Hometown: New York, NY (urban)
High School: Private all-female school, 45 students in graduating class
GPA: N/A (school doesn't have GPA)
SAT: 740 Math, 800 Verbal
Extracurriculars: Editor of literary magazine, head of political awareness committee, head of Asian awareness committee, took afternoon classes at the Metropolitan Museum of Art.
Summer Activities: Foreign exchange programs to France, taught English in Japan, interned for congresswoman's reelection campaign.
Awards: Silver Prize in scholastic writing, academic awards including English Prize, history prize, French prize, and analytic writing prize.
Family Background and Education: Her parents divorced when Sue was three, and her mother has a junior high–level education due to the Chinese Cultural Revolution.
Nationality/Ethnicity: Chinese
College Acceptances: Harvard (early admission)
College Rejections: None

As a young child, Sue Meng was always fascinated by art and literature. She grew up in New York City, where the dynamism and culture of the city offered her innumerable opportunities to explore her interests. However, she was lucky to be able to grow up in a place that nourished her intellectual interests. Sue was born in Beijing, China, and came to the United States when she was six and a half with her mother, who was a survivor of the Cultural Revolution. In New York, not only was she exposed to the city's cultural offerings, but she was able to take advantage of the academic ones as well. She participated in Prep for Prep, a talent search program for minority students in New York public schools to prepare them for the rigorous application process for New York City's exclusive private schools. For two years, she took enrichment courses after school and during summers, and in seventh grade was admitted to the Brearley School, an all-female institution, which she attended for the rest of her high school career.

High School

In high school, Sue discovered her passion for literature and writing. She was editor of her school's literary magazine and took afternoon classes at the Metropolitan Museum of Art, which were free to New York City high school students. Although she was very much involved in her school community as head of the political awareness committee and the Asian awareness committee, it was this program that she considered to be her most significant extracurricular experience on her Harvard application.

The Application and Essay

Sue carefully crafted her application so that it revealed two different sides of her. She was most proud of her primary essay, a non-fiction piece about her relationship with her grandfather and his fight with Parkinson's disease. It was a piece she had written for a creative writing class her junior year, not meant for a college essay, yet she believes that was the key to why her essay succeeded: because she was personal and human and heartfelt, she was able to reach her readers on an emotional level, which really made her application stand out.

Sue's second essay was about her experience at the Mountain School, which she participated in during her junior year. The Mountain School was a program that placed forty-five juniors on a farm. This opportunity "was an amazing learning experience," Sue says, which she emphasized in an essay that revealed her intellectual side, as she was able to convey the challenging and world-changing experiences she encountered at the Mountain School. In addition to her two essays, Sue also submitted a writing portfolio that really showcased her creative work in high school.

Contacts and Connections

As a senior, Sue applied to Harvard early action and was admitted. She considers herself extremely lucky to have been in a small high school community where she was able to establish a close relationship with her teachers and her college advisor, whom she relied on heavily throughout the college application process. Not only was her advisor crucial in providing her advice, but she also edited her essays. Because Sue did not have any contacts whatsoever with Harvard, her advisor's experience with past Harvard applicants was invaluable to her.

At Harvard

While at Harvard, Sue continued to explore her love of literature. She became a concentrator in history and literature and founded a journal of history and literature called *Historia*. In addition, she was an editorial columnist for *The Harvard Crimson*; was fiction editor for *The Advocate*, Harvard's literary magazine; and was on the Historical Committee for Harvard Model Congress. One summer, she wrote for the student-produced *Let's Go: China* travel guide as a researcher-writer. In addition, she worked part-time as a peer tutor at the Writing Center starting in her sophomore year. After she graduated, she began pursuing a Ph.D. at Oxford University as a Rhodes Scholar, although she was also selected for a Marshall Scholarship.

The Bottom Line

From her past experience with applying to colleges as well as fellowships, Sue emphasizes that the key to a successful application is honesty: "Try to just be yourself, in terms of not giving them what you think they want to hear, not the clichéd 'I surmounted this incredible challenge,' but by being as honest as you can. That will make the admissions officer have a better time reading the essay, and have the whole experience for you as enjoyable as possible."

—Casey Bi

Sarah A. Moran

Hometown: Clemmons, NC (rural)

High School: Public School, 600 students in graduating class

GPA: 4.0

SAT: 790 Math, 790 Verbal

Extracurriculars: President of the National Honor Society, Women in Politics club, student council secretary, varsity soccer team.

Summer Activities: Governor's School, soccer camp, waitressing at a local restaurant.

Awards: YWCA Women in Leadership Award, Montague Award (highest senior GPA), voted "most dedicated" by her peers.

Family Background and Education: Her mom graduated from University of Maryland as an undergrad and went to Georgetown Medical School, while her dad went to Holy Cross as an undergrad and also ended up at Georgetown Medical School. They are both doctors.

Nationality/Ethnicity: White

College Acceptances: Harvard, MIT, Georgetown, Columbia, Princeton, UNC Chapel Hill

College Rejections: None

Sarah A. Moran shows that persistence and dedication in the face of adversity can get you into college. In her conservative hometown, Sarah's liberal values alienated her from most of her classmates, but by being a leader inside and out of the classroom, Sarah was able to lend credibility to her ideology. By being a vocal opponent to the war in Iraq, Sarah placed herself in the minority, but at the same time was able to ameliorate the status of minority viewpoints and groups through her work with such student groups as the Women in Politics club. Sarah's dedication and drive are admirable qualities and ones that led her successfully into the college application process.

High School
In high school, Sarah showed her commitment to academic advancement as the president of the National Honor Society and served her school community as the student council secretary. "I was very outgoing in high school, as well as being genuinely interested in school," says Sarah. "I was friends with all of my teachers and guidance counselors." In addition to primary academic commitments, Sarah was a driving force in her school's Women in Politics club. Outside of the classroom, Sarah displayed athletic prowess as a member of the varsity soccer team. "I played sports, so a lot of people knew me," says Sarah. "But I had a pretty tight group of friends."

The Application and Essay
Sarah's application emphasized the dichotomy of her lifestyle by illustrating the frustrations and joys of being a liberal coming from a conservative hotbed. "People would dismiss my ideas fundamentally," says Sarah. She jokes that she still receives letters from her local church despite having differing views on the world. Her application attempted to highlight her commitment to social justice in a difficult environment. "There is nothing harder than arguing with someone who can't understand a different perspective," says Sarah. "I just had no support network outside of my teachers and some friends. I started angering people when I would speak up, especially my senior year."

Sarah made no qualms about being anti-establishment in her application essay. "I wrote my application about the problems of the College Board/AP system," Sarah says. "It is a monopoly and forces students into superficial learning." Sarah chose to receive no aid from parents, teachers, or friends on her essay. The idea for her essay came from the application process itself, which is a difficult but intriguing angle to take.

Contacts and Connections

Sarah had an interview, but no legacy status or connections to the school. Sarah's interview was very difficult. Her interviewer was a computer programmer at IBM and she claims she made a mistake of telling him that she took computer science. As a result he made her work through some code with him and then he asked her to work out a calculus problem: "So there is a cylinder, lying on its side, and it's filling up with water at x rate. At what time t will the water be ¾ of the way up the cylinder?" Aside from the math he asked her about her activities, and naturally they got into a political discussion about the war in Iraq and the Bush administration. "In total, my interview lasted over two hours!" says Sarah.

At Harvard

Despite moving from a conservative high school to Harvard's liberal breeding ground, Sarah has not lost her passion for activism. As an outspoken member of Harvard's progressive communities, Sarah is a leader in the Harvard AIDS forum and a quiet presence in her residential house. As a social studies concentrator, Sarah is able to combine her activism and social justice with her academic interests. She also enjoys being a prefect to first-year students, by organizing study breaks and acting as an advisor and mentor to students. Socially Sarah has mastered the art of avoiding the finals clubs and enjoying the Cambridge environs.

The Bottom Line

When asked what she would recommend to college applicants based on her experiences, Sarah says, "Be honest in your application, and try hard to emphasize why you are unique. Don't just do activities that will look good on your résumé, because the admissions people read the same things over and over again. Get involved with things you are truly interested in that will give you experiences that other applicants may not have."

—Adam P. Schneider

Kristen Tracey

Hometown: Armonk, NY (suburban)

High School: Private all-female school, 65 students in graduating class

GPA: 4.0

SAT: 800 Math, 800 Verbal

Extracurriculars: Math team, literary magazine, debate club, knitting club, cross-country team, graphic and design club, flutist.

Summer Activities: Intern at local publishing company, attended Harvard Summer School.

Awards: Math team county award, National Merit Finalist and Scholarship winner.

Family Background and Education: Kristen's mother, who is half-Japanese, attended Harvard as an undergraduate and later went on to New York University Law School. Her father completed his undergraduate degree at Cornell and also attended NYU Law.

Nationality/Ethnicity: Half Irish, quarter Japanese, and quarter French-Canadian.

College Acceptances: Harvard, Columbia, New York University, Wellesley, Vassar, University of Chicago

College Rejections: Yale

Entering the gates of Harvard Yard at the young age of seventeen, Kristen Tracey prides herself on being one of many "premature" Harvard students. She left her suburban New York high school a year early to join the Crimson and to give herself a challenge, she says. In high school, she was one of the most active members of her class and worked hard during her three years of high school to prove her readiness for college. Adept at science, math, and English, Kristen says she has often had difficulty in deciding what passion to pursue. A self-identified TV junkie, Kristen hopes to concentrate in film studies and to pursue a career in writing for television after graduation.

High School

Kristen attended an elite private women's high school just outside of New York City. In high school, she spent her time doing everything from math to music to sports. On her high school's math team, Kristen went on to win numerous local awards and competed with her team at the national level. Although math took up a major portion of her life, it was not her only passion. In between solving equations, Kristen found time to start a knitting club in her junior year of high school and joined the debate club to enhance her speaking skills. She also served as editor of her school's literary magazine throughout her high school career and made her mark in her school's graphic and design club during her freshman year. She also found time to practice the flute—a hobby she has enjoyed since age seven. Perfecting her image as the ultimate well-rounded student, Kristen participated in cross-country at her school for three years, eventually making it to the varsity team.

The Application and Essay

A second-generation Harvard student, Kristen heard a lot about Harvard from her mother, a Harvard graduate. She decided to apply with her mother's encouragement, having grown up hearing about the school's reputation.

Kristen says she listed her diverse roster of activities in a fairly ordinary manner. With the guidance of her school counselor, she included a supplementary short story that she had written for the school magazine to make her application stand out. "I thought the essay was actually pretty terrible, but everyone loved it," she says.

Kristen focused on her writing talents in her college application, moving her math and science capabilities to the background. "I was trying to emphasize my identity as a writer," she says. The only problem Kristen ran into was trying to live up to the expectations of a talented writer. "First, I had to write really good essays to convince them I was actually a writer," she says. Kristen started the creative process by writing about what she had done during each summer of her high school career. During her freshman summer, she interned at a local publishing company. After her sophomore year, Kristen attended Harvard's own summer school program. Kristen says she then created a repertoire of about twelve essays, but ended up using only three of them in the end. "I wrote about eight drafts of every single essay," she recalls. "It was blood and tears."

For her University of Chicago application, Kristen decided to take a different approach and submitted an essay about a recent trip to Japan. She wanted to make her essay unique and did so by centering her essay on eating a raw eggplant. For her NYU application, Kristen included an essay about the volunteer work she had done in her community and at school.

After getting feedback from her parents and guidance counselor, Kristen decided to submit an essay about the publishing internship she had completed over her freshman year with her common application that she would send off to Harvard. She made it unique by writing about all of the mistakes she had made on the first day of work and how she managed to prove herself after that point. Using this theme, Kristen was able to tell about an important experience and simultaneously emphasize her unrelenting and refined character. She ended her essay by tying this experience to her future and by detailing how her mistakes would craft her career and education plans. Kristen focused her two-paragraph extracurricular essay on her experience as editor of the school's literary magazine.

Contacts and Connections

Kristen's mother attended Harvard in the 1970s, but other than that, Kristen says she didn't meet or talk to anyone with ties to Harvard. Kristen also attended Harvard Summer School and included that information on Harvard's supplement to the common application.

At Harvard

After spending her high school years at an all-female school, Kristen says she has enjoyed the opportunity to hang out with members of the opposite sex at Harvard. Kristen says she likes the social scene that clubs at Harvard offer to students. Kristen continues to pursue her interests in English, writing for both Harvard's cinema magazine and the *Harvard Book Review*. In school, Kristen plans to continue her film studies major. She took on a job recently as a tutor with Boston public high school kids. But besides work and academics, Kristen says she is still able to fit in her coveted ten hours of TV per week.

The Bottom Line

Kristen recommends paying special attention to the desires of the admissions committee when completing an application. "I think it's just like the SATs—don't be yourself," she says. "Know what they want and give it to them." She also said it helps to build amicable relationships with high school staff—especially those who might potentially be writing a recommendation. "Be good to your teachers who will then give you a good recommendation," she says.

—Javier C. Hernandez

Anonymous Applicant

Hometown: Queens, NY (urban)
High School: Large public school, about 750 students in graduating class
GPA: 96/100
SAT: 800 Math, 750 Verbal
Extracurriculars: Co-concert mistress of symphony orchestra, co-editor of *Math Survey* magazine, editor of art magazine
Summer Activities: Telluride summer program, family trip to China, internship at investment firm, door-to-door salesperson for BJ's Wholesale Club.
Awards: Telluride Scholar, Chemistry Award, National Merit Scholarship.
Family Background and Education: Her parents met, married, and had her in Shanghai, China, before moving to the United States for graduate school. Her mother immigrated to the United States first to earn her

Ph.D. degree from Johns Hopkins University in biostatistics. She currently teaches and researches at Columbia. Her father also immigrated to the United States, to earn his MBA, and he currently works for MetLife.

Nationality/Ethnicity: Chinese-American

College Acceptances: Harvard, Cornell, University of Chicago, University of Michigan, SUNY Binghamton, Swarthmore

College Rejections: Yale (wait-listed)

This applicant came to the United States at the age of eight and entered the U.S. education system in the third grade. Every day of high school, she commuted for three hours between her home in Queens, New York, and her high school in Manhattan. She is not only enthusiastic, smart, and caring, but also diverse in what she has done and what she hopes to do.

High School

The applicant's high school career was filled with a variety of achievements. She finished her high school math requirements by the end of sophomore year and took advanced courses at New York University. She also worked as a intern for the investment company Weiss Peck & Greer and studied at the Art Students League of New York, where Jackson Pollock once took classes. She played the violin and was the co-concert mistress for her high school symphony. Outside of class, she worked for the China Institute, assisting exhibits of Chinese art and antiques. She also wrote articles in Chinese for *Mengya*, a monthly literature journal, including an essay on volunteerism in America. During the summer after her junior year, she was selected to participate in the Telluride Association Summer Program. At the University of Michigan, she took a six-week seminar on race, ethnicity, and gender in British-American history that inspired her to study social relations.

The Application and Essay

Outside of guidance from her English teacher, she undertook her application by herself. Her English teacher was also one of her recommenders—having been a source of support and guidance. She found most of the application to Harvard easy to complete, but she spent two to three weeks working on the two essays she submitted. She started both of them afresh and completed three drafts for each. Having written longer essays for English and fiction-writing courses, she felt prepared to undertake these essays.

Her first essay focused on the problems of art, a series of questions that she had entertained and struggled with throughout high school. Inspired by musician and music educator David Mannes's autobiography *Music Is My Faith*, her essay considered her simultaneous desire to create art and her lingering reservations about certain ethical obligations that art did not fulfill.

Her second essay described memories of her childhood with a feeling of nostalgia. It didn't aim to convey any direct message, but depicted the experiences of an immigrant child focusing specifically on the image of trees from her childhood in Shanghai. The essay grew from a creative inspiration she had had in response to an essay question on the University of Chicago application. She began the essay with a quote from Carl Jung's *Memories, Dreams, Reflections* in which Jung compares trees to God's thoughts. After working on her essay for several weeks, she showed it to her English teacher. She sent this essay to Harvard as well as the University of Chicago, and Chicago's Dean of Admissions wrote personally to tell her how much he liked her essay.

Her application focused on the way in which she was an unorthodox student at her high school. Because the school and its students were more focused on math and science, she wanted to show her abilities as a writer and humanitarian. Because many students had competitive GPAs, she did not feel like she had an especially good chance of being accepted.

Contacts and Connections

Without any insider connections, the only contact she had with Harvard was through her two alumni interviews at the Harvard Club in New York City. Before enrolling, she had visited Harvard only once on a trip to Boston with her family in sixth grade. Although she knew a couple of graduates from her high school at Harvard, she did not know them well enough to ask for advice.

At Harvard

Since coming to college, she has written for *The Crimson* Arts section, worked as a research assistant at the Weatherhead Center as well as the Radcliffe Institute for Advanced Study, and interned at the American Repertory Theater. She is co-president of Harvard China Care, a university organization that aims to improve the lives of Chinese orphans by sending volunteers overseas, fundraising, and coordinating a playgroup for adopted children in Boston. She spent part of her sophomore summer at an orphanage in northern China, and also worked as a writer for the travel guide *Let's Go: China*.

The Bottom Line

To those who are following in her footsteps, she says, "My first impulse was to say 'be yourself,' very cliché, but true. Then I realized that many of us don't know ourselves enough to 'be ourselves.' So I guess better advice would be to be as open-minded as possible, try to welcome new experiences if you can, and try to enjoy them."

—Yan Fang

Strategy 7: Make and Use Connections

Not everyone who applies to Harvard is the daughter of a senator, the son of a wealthy donor, or the nephew of the dean of admissions. Don't despair if you don't already have connections going into the process. The applicants featured in this chapter forged relationships with Harvard admissions interviewers and others who encouraged them to apply and guided them through the process. Taking the time to meet with admissions officials or local Harvard alumni can give you an edge and convince the admissions office that you're serious and excited about Harvard.

Forging a connection with Harvard can take as little as a trip to Cambridge to meet with an admissions officer. This will help ensure that those reading your application will remember you; you'll be a face instead of just another file. If you can't make it to Cambridge, though, try to connect and keep in touch with your alumni interviewer. These people, often recent Harvard grads and/or prominent members of the local community, can answer your questions about Harvard and can be your advocates, since the local alumni group makes recommendations to the admissions office. Admissions officers make informational visits to high schools around the country—so do your best to attend. Many successful applicants got to know the people deciding on their application at such sessions.

Although whom you draw as your alumni interviewer can sometimes be a matter of luck, anyone can try to forge a connection with an admissions officer. If your officer is coming to an informational session near you, don't hesitate to speak to him or her after the session or ask questions about Harvard and your application. If you feel like your alumni interview went particularly well, or you connected or shared a common interest with this person, make sure to follow up and keep in touch.

As you try to make the most of your contacts and connections, consider the following tips:

- *Prepare for your interview.* Practice answers to questions you're expecting, and also think about questions to ask your interviewer about the school beforehand. It's important to communicate enthusiasm.
- Attend local information sessions and try to meet with the admissions officer afterward.
- If you can visit the campus before you apply, try to meet with admissions officers. Don't be overly pushy, though, which is a huge turn-off.
- Be enthusiastic in all your dealings with alumni and admissions officers. You never know when you'll hit it off and gain a mentor for the admissions process.

Gerardo Con Diaz

Hometown: San José, Costa Rica (urban)
High School: Private school, 100 students in graduating class
GPA: 4.6 (weighted)
SAT: 790 Math, 650 Verbal
Extracurriculars: Math competitions, singing opera, coaching math teams.
Summer Activities: Teaching social studies to deaf children.
Awards: First place in age group at National Math Competition, First place at May Iebro Math Competition, Bronze at the Central American Math Competition.
Family Background and Education: Father is Chinese; he has a B.A. from Louisiana State University in civil engineering and is a shoestore owner. Mother is Costa Rican; she owns a day-care center and didn't attend college.

Nationality/Ethnicity: Chinese–Costa Rican
College Acceptances: Harvard (early admission)
College Rejections: None

Gerardo Con Diaz is a happy-go-lucky math whiz who takes great joy out of the things in life that are simple to him: an afternoon doing math problems in the library, singing classical tunes as he walks to class, or talking to friends over a good meal. In the midst of math finals, he will appear unphased—perhaps excited—to accept his upcoming challenges. His personal philosophy? To "eat, smile, and work."

High School

Ask Gerardo what he loves about math, and he'll tell you, in a dramatic voice, "I love math with all my heart because I feel it is one of the few truly perfect things that we can get close to. I've always thought of mathematics as something that rests above us and of mathematicians as the ones who actually try to pull down from it." In seventh grade, he competed in his first math contest ever, and remembers telling his father after the event, "This is what I want to do for the rest of my life." He won several prestigious math competitions during high school, including top prize at the National Math Competition and silver and bronze medals at the May Iebro American Competition. After eleventh grade and his graduation from high school (because of Costa Rican school schedules), he took a year off to coach math teams involved in the competitions at which he excelled. His most stressful moments came on his job as national tutor for one team, when he was "legally in charge of three teenagers, and had to defend their scores in front of an international jury," he says. "I knew the kids because I had been teaching them geometry for months, but having a group of mathematicians tear apart their arguments expecting that I will justify even seemingly insignificant mistakes was perhaps the most pressure I have ever had because of the contests. At the end, they won a top score and two bronze medals."

Gerardo also pursued his love of music and singing, especially opera, which he cultivated in high school as a soloist for the school choir, a bass baritone for graduations and other ceremonies at a local arts high school, and a member of a group of friends who sang at churches around the country. "I have always said that doing mathematics is my passion, but singing is the life that allows me to keep going," he says. He got the lead in a musical in sixth grade and landed a spot in the high school's choir (which was best in its category in all of Central America) when he was in seventh grade. "I joined a local opera choir in 2001 and the vocal coach heard me and offered to work with me. I discovered that learning how to use my voice in a song is one of the most rewarding experiences I have had," he explains. "I love studying voice because it is hypnotizing. Learning to control your voice means learning how to not think about it. It means becoming one with your body and just letting the sound come out. It is interesting how through seemingly artificial and counterintuitive processes, a singer gets to express such an organic relationship with music."

The Application and Essay

Gerardo applied to Harvard after eleventh grade but was wait-listed and rejected. "I had no college counselors," he says, "and I knew no one who had applied to a U.S. school." His recommenders didn't speak English, he says, and their letters were only a paragraph long. During his year off after applying, he wrote a mathematics research topic about sequential compactness. He wanted future admissions officers to "know that I could sit down for long hours and do math and that I was happy doing that," he says. He cleaned up his application and wrote mostly about his love of mathematics and opera.

Each of Gerardo's essays went through five drafts. His first essay focused on the sequential compactness project he completed. "I emphasized the independence of the project, how I hadn't had a math lecture in four years and still managed to write a research paper on basic real analysis because of work I had done independently," he says. The second essay talked about teaching the alphabet to a deaf girl, when he spent one summer teaching social studies to deaf kids. The essay was "very hard to write because I wanted it to be full of feelings without being cheesy or fake," he explains. "The entire piece was like a short story followed by a personal comment about how I felt about it." Gerardo's teachers and financial admissions officer Robert Clagett (see "Contacts and Connections") helped fine-tune his essays. "Since English is my second language, they made sure that I made no stupid mistakes and let me know exactly when the essay left the impression I wanted it to leave," Gerardo remembers.

Contacts and Connections

Robert Clagett worked at Gerardo's high school as a college counselor during Gerardo's year off and then became a financial admissions officer at Harvard just in time for Gerardo to reapply. Eventually, Clagett became Gerardo's good friend as well. "I had never written an essay in my life until my senior year, and he was the patient man who read the first words that came out of my word processor," Gerardo says. "These first words were a very bad draft of a college essay and he gave me ideas and taught me about style so that I could improve my work." Clagett even critiqued some of Gerardo's recordings of arias he had done.

Gerardo met Lori Glazer, his admissions officer at Harvard, at an information session in his area. He remembers her as "patient and encouraging," adding that "the great thing about admissions officers here is that they really want to get to know the applicants, and they take their time to do it." Gerardo also had great success with interviews— all three of them. He had two interviews with alumna Renata Villers, with whom he remembers having a strong connection and a long conversation. His third interview with a mathematician was "intense," he says. The interviewer took out a list of concepts Gerardo had claimed to understand, showed him a piece of paper, and said to Gerardo, "It says here that you have taught Euclidean plane transformations to national teams. Would you tell me about them?" Gerardo loved the interview and felt a strong connection with him as well.

When Gerardo was wait-listed, he didn't appeal, since he felt he knew "exactly what went wrong," he says. "All I did was ask what I could do better and then did it. I think of my first application as a practice one." He took a year off, sang and studied math daily, and focused on finding "what I really wanted from life."

At Harvard

So far at Harvard he is keeping busy taking upper-level math courses (like honors multivariable calculus and linear algebra, classical geometry, and complex analysis), taking singing lessons after applying and receiving a subsidy from Harvard's Office for the Arts. He was in the choir for *Don Giovanni* but had to quit. "Harvard is a great place" to cultivate his interests in math and singing, he says, adding, "I love it here not only because of its warmth and friendliness, but because it's a great place to finally give my life to the things I love."

The Bottom Line

His advice about the admissions process is that "It's the one time you have a chance to brag. It's easy to try to be humble and to give yourself less credit than you deserve. When you do that, the admissions officers just have a piece of paper. They think that's all you have. You have to be absolutely honest and show off. It's not so much what you have as how you put it."

—*Katie M. Gray*

Max Newman

Hometown: Fairbanks, AK (rural outskirts/small city)
High School: Public school, about 300 students in graduating class
GPA: 4.3
SAT: 710 Math, 720 Verbal

Extracurriculars: Avid musician on guitar, tenor banjo, mandolin; jazz piano from age eleven; contra dancing; earth club president (environmental and school recycling).

Summer Activities: Worked as a gardener/janitor at Alaskaland, a theme park.

Awards: None.

Family Background and Education: Father got his B.A. in psychology from UC Berkeley, and his mother had some college experience at the University of Alaska–Fairbanks but never earned a diploma.

Nationality/Ethnicity: White

College Acceptances: Harvard, University of Chicago, Georgetown, Swarthmore, Oberlin, Washington University

College Rejections: None.

Max Newman is rarely seen without his trademark big brown fedora, which he wears over his very long, untamed curly brown hair. He hails from a rural area just outside of Fairbanks, Alaska. Max says that he did not know very much about colleges or the application process at all when he was applying, and he was also concerned about his relative lack of club activities and summer job experience. Max was no slouch, however. He invested, and still invests, a great deal of time into his passion: music.

High School

Max is mostly interested in Irish bluegrass, folk, and traditional music, along with the North American and European fiddle traditions. He plays the guitar, mandolin, tenor banjo, and piano, and is an avid contra dancer. (Contra is a form of American folk dance with moves similar to square dancing, but quite different in style.)

He spent a lot of time contra dancing and playing music for contra dances in high school. These dances were held twice a month, and he played at about a quarter to a third of them. He played with all sorts of bands, young and old. The group that danced regularly was about eighty to a hundred strong, but that wasn't nearly enough for Max. He said that he was "kind of a zealot" in terms of getting more young people into contra dancing. Max received a personal e-mail from an admissions officer at Harvard asking him to bring contra dancing to the Harvard community. Max was happy to oblige—he contra dances nearly every Thursday night at the VFW in Cambridge, and a sizable group of Harvard contra dancers, with their own Facebook group, goes with him.

During the fall and summer, and at other times during the year as well, Max loved to drive (and ferry) down to music festivals in Juneau. "Three years of high school, we did that," Max says. The twenty-hour drives and the ensuing music festivals would take about a week, and Max enjoyed that time hanging out with his friends, just playing music. And play music Max did. He would jam with his buddies once or twice every weekend, playing with bands ranging from acid rock to the bluegrass and traditional music that is his specialty.

Music is not all that Max did in high school. He was also the president of the earth club, which had the difficult task of coordinating the recycling effort in Fairbanks.

The Application and Essay

According to Max, he applied to Harvard "on a whim" because it was one of the few interesting schools with early action. He did not purposely conceive a theme for his application, but because he had been thinking a lot about communities of people at that point in his life, that theme ended up coming through. He emphasized his group activities and wrote about communities in his essay. When he was visiting the schools he applied to, his visits happened to fall near the deadlines of the applications, so Max handed in two of his applications by hand: Harvard's and Georgetown's. "It was just sort of more convenient, that I happened to be there at the right time," Max says. "I don't think it helped." The people he handed his application to did not introduce themselves or follow up with him.

Max wrote more essays than he was really supposed to, and greatly exceeded his word limit. His parents helped him edit his essays. He wrote one essay listing his extracurricular activities, but it was mostly an essay about contra dancing. He also wrote about going to a sauna with a bunch of his friends. He describes this as "the naked essay," in which he discussed "an odd but very natural" and "shamelessly naked" experience with a group of people of many different ages and races. He wrote about how the group of people transcended their differences while taking part in this communal, naked activity. He felt strongly about it, and thought it would add "off-the-wall value" to the application and would get him noticed.

However, he later heard from his admissions officer that that was not what got him noticed. Max also wrote about his experience with Boys State, in which he, a liberal from Alaska, hung out with a bunch of "scary, intense army guys." He wrote a bit about politics in this essay, and included a line about how politicians shake hands and kiss babies "but should never shake babies or kiss hands."

"[My parents] told me I should take that line out because they said that it was a little too goofy," Max says. "But my admissions officer, Jake, laughed, which is apparently not an easy thing to accomplish for a tired admissions officer at one in the morning."

Overall, Max did not see his essays as a very important part of his application. "I think it is very hard to write an actual essay that's not conceited," Max says. "So you shouldn't worry about writing a conceited essay. No matter what you do, it's going to be conceited. All admissions essays are terrible. Which is why admissions officers get paid so much. No essay is ever finished, it's just due, as my English teacher used to say. Don't worry."

Contacts and Connections

Max met his admissions officer, Jacob Kaufman, when the officer visited Max's high school, and he helped inspire Max to apply. Another person who spurred Max to apply was William Fitzsimmons, the director of admissions at Harvard. They never actually met, but Max drove to Anchorage to hear him give a presentation along with admissions officers from other universities. Max described him as "impressive," and said that "[his presentation] probably inspired me to apply more than anything else."

Max had his interview at a local coffee shop in Fairbanks. He describes the interview as very relaxed, "very chill." Oddly enough, he had his interview less than a week before he received his acceptance. He did not follow up with his interviewer, or vice versa. There wasn't any time.

At Harvard

At Harvard, Max is the vice president of both the Alaska Klub and the Celtic club, which he calls "figurehead" positions. He also contra dances nearly every Thursday night at the Cambridge VFW, and there is a small but loyal (and unofficial) contingent of contra dancers who go with him.

The Bottom Line

"Applying to college can be a terrible experience or an awful one. You choose," Max bemoans half-jokingly. However, he admits that "it will all end up all right." His main advice is to "take your application seriously, but not too seriously. Because if you're not having any fun with it, then your admissions officer won't have any fun reading it. Don't try to be like me or anyone else in this book. Just be yourself, and all will be well."

—*William L. Jusino*

Sutha Satkunarajah

Hometown: Kingston, London, U.K. (suburban)
High School: Private all-male grammar school, 175 students in graduating class
GPA: No assigned GPA
SAT: 650 Math, 680 Verbal

Extracurriculars: Managing director of Young Enterprise, president of British Association of Young Scientists, prefect, vice captain of Livingstone House team.

Summer Activities: Externship at Novartis pharmaceutical company.

Awards: Harvard Book Prize, Duke of Edinburgh Silver, British Biology Olympiad Gold.

Family Background and Education: Father and mother did not attend university.

Nationality/Ethnicity: Sri Lankan

College Acceptances: Harvard, Cambridge

College Rejections: None

Sutha Satkunarajah is a long way from home. After a childhood spent traveling between Doha, Qatar, and London, at age thirteen, following his parents' divorce, Sutha relocated permanently with his mother and younger sister to a suburb of London. He grew up in a single-parent, working-class family and credits his mother's experience for fostering the drive which brought him to Harvard. "Watching her grow as a young and naïve foreigner in an new place, handling the burdens of being a single parent, taught me true integrity and perseverance. Her troubles fueled my desire to be a 'working-class' hero," he says.

High School

In high school at the Tiffin School for Boys, a selective day school, Sutha found himself among others of a similar socioeconomic group. "Being among others who were also smart and not necessarily wealthy created a stimulating ethos: We all wanted to utilize our talents to improve the welfare of our personal lives, as well as that of the world," he says of his high school environment. As one of about 175 students in his year, he had plenty of opportunities to develop the skills to do so.

Sutha held a number of leadership positions, including the managing director of a company of twenty-five in a national Young Enterprise program that held a fashion show during his lower sixth form, serving as a prefect in upper sixth form, and as vice captain of his house team in school athletic competitions. His primary interest, however, was the natural sciences. "In my application, I painted myself as a research scientist," he says. This interest was developed by an externship at the Swiss pharmaceutical company Novartis and his work as president of the school's chapter of the British Association of Young Scientists. When the time came to consider universities, he chose to apply to Cambridge rather than Oxford because of its strength in the natural sciences. "Harvard doesn't enter the consciousness of the average Brit," he says.

While he was one of a score of students in his form to win acceptance to Oxbridge, Sutha was only one of two applicants to Harvard. He says of his decision to consider school in the United States, "I had an American substitute teacher once who suggested considering it, and, although I am ashamed to admit it, part of it was the influence of movies like *American Pie* and *Road Trip*. I think there are three kinds of Brits who apply to Harvard: the Americans studying abroad, the British who have long connections to the university, and the curious Brits."

The Application and Essay

For his application, Sutha chose to focus his essay on his family experience and its impact on his life. His background, and the motivation it gave him to achieve, were the major points of his essay. Unlike his application to Cambridge, he worked without the guidance of a counselor. Though he was the recipient of his school's Harvard Book Prize during the lower sixth form, he had only one contact with the university during the application process.

Contacts and Connections

"I was fortunate to have someone very respected within the Harvard community as my interviewer," Sutha says, "a former president of the Harvard Alumni Association. Once he heard that I had gotten twelve A's for GCSEs (a standard British placement exam offered in the sophomore year) and that I had received a matriculation offer to study at

Christ's College, Cambridge, our interview shifted gears, and we started discussing the merits of Harvard over Cambridge. The interview lasted a good many hours. I would advise anyone to keep up with their interviewer; Jim and I have worked on the Annual British Students Dinner at Harvard for two years now."

Following his acceptance at Harvard, he faced a difficult decision between pursuing a natural sciences degree at Cambridge or coming to Harvard to pursue biochemistry. "Pre-frosh weekend was a good sell," he said. "My host took me to Eleganza, a big campus fashion show, and I saw Tatyana Ali and Natalie Portman in the audience. Where else can you get that?"

At Harvard

Sutha ultimately chose Harvard because he felt it was a different and more interesting path from the one taken by the rest of his classmates. The transition to American college life was not as easy as portrayed in the typical American college movie. "The British mentality at college is to mess around your first two years, then buckle down," he says. Under the British university system, students focus on a single area of study during a three-year program. "I definitely struggled with the constant assessment at first. For example, during my freshman writing course, Southern Writers Reconsidered, other students had all this knowledge of geography and of the American writers, which I lacked. Sophomore year, I finally buckled down."

Despite some early difficulties with the American system, Sutha also found some benefits to a liberal arts education. "A big merit of Harvard is the ease with which you can change your area of study," he says. Over four years, he has switched concentrations from biochemistry to psychology, and then to cognitive neuroscience, and next year will be working at a major management consulting firm in New York City. Though he has no regrets about his choice to attend an American university, he also gives some credit to Cambridge: "I think my acceptance there had a lot to do with my being accepted at Harvard."

The Bottom Line

Sutha says, "I think that there is definitely some luck in the application process. I think it's very important whom you get as your interviewer. The only other applicant in my class had an alumni interviewer with whom he didn't connect very well, and he was unfortunately not accepted." Making use of a key connection, and the resources and information they can provide, can be a significant help in the application process.

—*Ashley B. T. Ma*

Minhua Zhang

Hometown: Shanghai, China

High School: Public boarding school, 400 students in graduating class

GPA: No GPA assigned

SAT: 800 Math, 550 Verbal

Extracurriculars: President of student council for two years, member of debate team.

Summer Activities: Swimming camps, science summer school, travel with family.

Awards: First prize in National Physics Olympiad (Shanghai region), second prize in National Mathematics Olympiad (Shanghai region), first prize in American Mathematics Olympiad, first prize in Rado Chinese Youth Talent Search, second prize in U.S. Physics Bowl, championship in Shanghai High School debating contest.

Family Background and Education: His mother is a professor of physical chemistry at Fudan University in Shanghai and his father is a professor of education management at Fudan University, as well as the university's vice president.

Nationality/Ethnicity: Chinese

College Acceptances: Harvard, Swarthmore, University of Chicago, Princeton, MIT, Cornell, University of Rochester, Drexel, Washington University

College Rejections: Caltech, Columbia

An undisputed math and science talent with a strong background in the humanities, Minhua Zhang may not have even needed that extra little push to cinch his admission. But it came nevertheless, and from the unlikeliest source. Although he had no connections or contacts at Harvard, Minhua ended up with an alumni interviewer he really clicked with. Not only was he able to impress the interviewer with his own background, but the alumnus was able to sell Minhua on Harvard—an important point, since the comfort factor is so important for international students.

High School

Minhua was a member of a special class at Fudan High School that was recruited for an accelerated science program. After completing regular sciences in one year, he studied university-level sciences during the rest of high school. During that time, he won a range of prestigious academic awards, including first prize in National Physics Olympiad (Shanghai region), second prize in National Mathematics Olympiad (Shanghai region), first prize of Rado Chinese Youth Talent Search, and second prize in the U.S. Physics Bowl.

In addition to being a physics and math star, he also wrote and published articles and poetry. He wrote over twenty articles for newspapers, including the *Qingnian Bao* and the Chinese *Youth Daily*, and his poem in English about the return of the city Macao to China won the award for best composition in *English Weekly*. Minhua was also the president of the student council, a body responsible for all student activities that took place in school. He played the guitar, swam at Fudan University, and played on the basketball and ping-pong teams.

After completing high school in China, Minhua was one of the two Chinese students selected to participate in an exchange program at Sidwell Friends High School in Washington, D.C. He decided to apply to American universities during that year, and after arriving in D.C. in August 2000, he took the SAT exam during his second month in the States, the SAT Subject Tests during his third month, and applied for college during the fourth month. Although he had studied English since the end of primary school in China, improving his language skills for the SAT proved to be one of the most difficult tasks in America. During the year at Sidwell Friends, he completed all his science homework during the day, so that he could spend extra time completing his work for his American Studies course and studying for the verbal portions of the SAT at night. The end result was that he scored very well on the TOEFL exam that international students must take in order to apply to college in the United States.

The Application and Essay

Without any connections to the college, the most important aspects of Minhua's application were his talents in mathematics and physics and his well-rounded range of activities. He worked on his application intensely for a month and chose to include recommendations from two teachers from Sidwell Friends and one recommendation from a professor at Fudan University.

The essay was the most difficult portion of the application for Minhua, and he undertook a great deal of introspection in order to realize and describe his personal strengths and weaknesses. His essay focused on his personal growth as president of the student council at Fudan High School. "Student council was half my life," says Minhua. "What I learned about interpersonal relationships shapes how I see the people around me today." In his essay, Minhua described several scenarios that arose during his tenure in which his opinion differed from those of his colleagues on the student council. Many of these situations required immediate decisions, and Minhua solved the conflicts by laying out his personal logic and simultaneously synthesizing others' valuable points of view. Minhua learned from the multiplicity of solutions offered by other students, as well as the value of good working relations and showing respect to others. Because English is not his first language, Minhua asked his host family to read his essay and help him edit it.

Contacts and Connections

After submitting his application, Minhua had an alumni interview with the general manager of *The Washington Times*. His interview was quite enjoyable and lasted for over two hours, during which he had the opportunity to learn a lot about Harvard. His interviewer enjoyed talking to applicants and was extremely patient in listening to Minhua, who believes his English was difficult to understand at that time. Despite being extremely nervous before the meeting, Minhua felt encouraged by his interviewer and felt confident about his application after completing the interview.

At Harvard

Minhua majored in physics and mathematics, and in his free time he worked on the *Harvard China Review* and served as a course assistant for Math 21a, Math 21b, and Physics 1b. He is on the Leverett ping-pong team as well as the ballroom dance team, which is how he met his fiancée. After graduation, he plans to work as a hedge fund strategist in New York City.

The Bottom Line

Minhua says, "Do whatever you like, but try very hard to become the best at it. Many believe there is a generic formula to knock open Harvard's door, but the only 'formula' is to be differently talented from all others, to be a unique you."

—*Yan Fang*

Strategy 8: Make Yourself Heard and Campaign to Win

For most applicants, direct contact with college admissions offices is rare—not all schools require one-on-one interviews, and the Internet has largely revolutionized the way prospective students deal with the people in whose hands rest their own future. But not everybody has a smooth path to the gates of higher education—some students have to take their application process to the next level and personally advocate for their own admission. Addressing the admissions office personally isn't a cry of desperation—it's an excellent way to demonstrate one's commitment to the school, showing persistence, courage, and forthrightness. Admissions officers will certainly appreciate, if not reward, your efforts and your drive.

Different situations, of course, demand different strategies. Brad Michael Smith and Connor C. Wilson were both high school athletes and all-around achievers who found themselves on the verge of not attending Harvard at all. One fought hard for entrance following a Harvard deferral, the other turned Harvard down only to change his mind at the last second. But both took matters into their own hands and spent countless hours talking to admissions officers, coaches, and administrators in order to secure their spot at Harvard.

Do you worry that your candidacy will be lost in a sea of applications, that admissions offices will not be able to appreciate what you can offer? Do you feel that your interpersonal skills might help give you an edge in the process? If the admissions replies have come in and they are negative, do you think you were unjustly overlooked? Is there more you have to say? Going the next step and contacting the admissions office directly requires courage and tact, but if you do find yourself in this position, consider the following advice:

- *Stay enthusiastic!* In all your communications with the admissions office and anyone associated with the university, make sure you and any of your advocates project the right tone—enthusiasm and eagerness, not frustration, indignation, or desperation.
- If you are on the waiting list and you are hoping to get off, it is always a good idea to ask for new recommendations from somebody whose letter was not used on your regular application.
- Try to put a face to your name by sending slides and letters, going to visit the admissions office in person, or setting up individual interviews.
- *Consult your college counselor.* More than anyone else, he or she can help organize a push for admission and lobby on your behalf.

Brad Michael Smith

Hometown: Knoxville, TN (suburban)
High School: Private school, 400 students in graduating class
GPA: 4.32
SAT: not taken, ACT: 35
Extracurriculars: Class president of student government association, president of government and politics association, editor-in-chief of yearbook, captain of Mock Trial team, co-captain of fellowship of Christian athletes, counsul-at-large of Junior Classical League, chairman of ambassadors club, Younglife/Campaigners, Knoxville Bridge Builders, Model United Nations.
Summer Activities: Spent summers playing tennis and doing water sports.
Awards: United States Presidential Scholar, National Merit Scholarship Award winner.
Family Background and Education: His father got his master's degree in engineering at the University of Tennessee, and his mother got her M.D.D. there as well.
Nationality/Ethnicity: White

College Acceptances: Harvard, Washington University, Furman, Davidson, Vanderbilt, Duke, Wake Forest
College Rejections: None

"I didn't want to come here: I just applied because it was Harvard," says
Brad Smith about the start of his college decision process. "I didn't try
very hard on the application." A true Southerner, his college applications mostly ranged into no colder climate than that of North Carolina.
Applying to Harvard had never been a priority or long-term goal for him.

A government concentrator, he has always had a strong interest in
serving the public, though he also hopes to achieve a balanced life.
Reaching the second goal has sometimes proved difficult in the face of
his other ambitions, as far back as high school.

High School

"Freshman year, I got involved with a lot of activities, and stayed involved through high school," Brad says. "It was a small school, so it
was easy to be involved." His interests included the yearbook, the
Mock Trial team, the Model UN club, the fellowship of Christian athletes, and student government. "I also did about four hundred hours of
community service. We did Habitat for Humanity, canned food drives,
and organized a dance for mentally disabled adults. We also raised
money for Child Help International."

By senior year, Brad had extensive leadership experience, serving
as editor of the yearbook, captain of the Mock Trial team and the fellowship of Christian athletes, and president of his class for all four
years. He was also valedictorian, and a U.S. Presidential Scholar.

The Application and Essay

Through his work in community service, Brad built up a desire to study
medicine and become a doctor. "I really wanted to be directly helping
people," he says. Focusing on this interest, his application emphasized
his coursework in the sciences and AP-level courses. As well, he dis-

cussed his experience shadowing an orthopedic surgeon for two years, exploring one interesting area of medicine.

"In my essay, I included an anecdote about how helping a classmate with a broken foot on a school trip sparked my interest in being a doctor," Brad says of his application. An English teacher who was also a Harvard alumnus helped him craft the essay and application. Brad's application won him acceptance at all the schools to which he applied.

After being offered a full scholarship to Washington University's undergraduate medical program, Brad turned down Harvard and planned on heading off to Missouri. "If I had really wanted to be a doctor, for me it would have been the place to go," he says. "But towards the end of my senior year, because of my experience doing some more government-organized programs, I started developing an interest in politics and moving in that direction."

"I turned down Harvard, and then I had second thoughts after graduation and changed my mind," he says. "The committee said they never overturn second decisions. Typically they find out that students who retract their rejections are more likely to be bad students." His mother and guidance counselor both sought out the admissions committee and lobbied successfully on his behalf.

Contacts and Connections

Brad himself had little contact with Harvard while applying. "I had a short interview with a local alumnus living in Knoxville, but other than that I had never seen Harvard until pre-frosh weekend," he says. "When I was trying to regain my acceptance, I never spoke with the admissions committee. They called for my mother and let her know about the decision."

His change in undergraduate plans was matched by a subsequent change in his plan of study. "Since I was turning down Washington University's medical school, my experience in public service and policy groups directed me toward studying government," he says. In college, this interest also led to involvement with many different political and policy groups.

At Harvard

Certain groups, such as Social Good Through Politics, a Social Security reform group Brad co-founded, adhere to his original goal of directly affecting and helping others. He has also maintained his community service work as a counselor with the Mission Hill After-School Program. "I know that formulating public policies can sometimes seem impersonal," he says, "but these policies create places like Mission Hill, and provide resources for that kind of after-school. Seeing how they affect the lives of people like my students inspires me to want to commit my life to developing effective public policies."

Brad's tendency to keep busy is also fed by his roles as chairman of the Massachusetts Alliance of College Republicans, member of the College National Republican Committee, Institute of Politics Student Advisory Board, and intern or assistant on several campaigns. Particularly close to his heart is Social Security reform, and the groups that deal closely with it.

After graduation, he plans to return to Tennessee and continue pursuing better reforms and policies to help people.

The Bottom Line

Brad credits a laid-back philosophy for helping him throughout the college application process. "The best thing is not to stress too much. There's not much you can do about it," he says.

—Ashley B. T. Ma

Connor C. Wilson

Hometown: Lone Tree, CO (suburban)
High School: Public school, 420 students in graduating class
GPA: 3.9
SAT: 720 Math, 750 Verbal

Extracurriculars: Student government representative, peer counselor, freshman orientation program, cross-country and track and field teams, the Student Advisory Group.

Summer Activities: Tour of Europe with International Sports Tours to race in seven different countries over about three weeks, Colorado Boys State, American Legion Boys Nation, part-time job in a restaurant.

Awards: Presidential Leadership Award, cross-country and track MVP.

Family Background and Education: His mother, one of eight children, received her B.A. degree from Ohio State. Connor's father got his undergraduate degree from the University of Delaware and then went for an M.B.A. at Dartmouth University's Tuck School of Business.

Nationality/Ethnicity: Scotch- and Irish-American

College Acceptances: Harvard, Boston College, University of Pennsylvania, Duke

College Rejections: Princeton, UNC, Georgetown, Cornell (wait-listed), Dartmouth (wait-listed), University of Virginia (wait-listed)

Connor is a runner, as you can tell just from seeing the man, but he is far from a simplistic joke caricature. He can slip from schoolboy teasing to passionate intellectual discussion about the most pressing political issues to excitement over his high score at the video game Halo without missing a beat. Although having a conservative ideology at Harvard puts him in somewhat of the minority at least vocally, if not intellectually, Connor continues to propound his views without ever seeming overly dogmatic. Connor was and continues to be an athlete with depth and a willingness to be himself.

High School

While at high school, Connor was involved in a variety of activities that are emblematic of his diversity of interests. Within his school, he was involved in student government, peer counseling, and LINK, the freshman orientation program. But most of all, Connor was always an athlete. He was well known to be the backbone of the cross-country and track and field teams throughout high school. Connor's devotion to the team shaped his style and attitude toward the well-rounded character that Harvard eventually recognized. It was leadership skills and ability to work well with others as part of a team that led Connor to the Student Advisory Group, a local student advisory panel that engaged in dialogue with the district administrators. With this diversity of talents it is not surprising how well-respected Connor was by his peers.

The Application and Essay

Understanding that many Harvard applicants had similarly stellar academic records, Connor tried to focus on his leadership skills and political leanings. As Connor remembers, "I did my best to emphasize my leadership skills and positions, my intent to further continue such leadership in college, and a subtle connection to my interest in politics."

In order to further demonstrate his depth, Connor wrote his essay on "my last Sunday long run with a friend that was leaving for college." This had been a tradition they had shared for a long time and this reflected both his own ability to deal with change and his understanding of the college process. Like many people, Connor does his best thinking in unusual places: "I got the idea in the shower." To make sure it was up to snuff, Connor had "two teachers, my mother, and a friend give me advice on it."

Contacts and Connections

Connor did not know anyone at Harvard at the beginning of his application process, but he certainly did by the end. Initially, Connor's application and interview were not impressive enough: he got deferred. Although Connor remembers "being very nervous for [his] first interview," his impression on leaving was "that it had gone very well." This impression was because the "interviewer seemed interested and engaged." A big part of Connor's self-satisfaction was rooted in the preparation he had made prior to the interview. "I had made sure to find out as much about him as I could—his career, his interests, how he liked Harvard."

After going through the process at a few other schools, however, Connor became less sure of how well his interview had gone. "After I had interviewed with other colleges I realized that I might have bombed it—I had talked politics, which I was interested in but not wholly informed on, I was slightly fidgety, and I didn't go in knowing enough about the school." Later, Connor found out "my interviewer really liked me. We have great conversations now at the summer barbecues and it's actually been a very nice relationship." But it wasn't enough to put him over the top in the competitive world of early admissions. He took the news in stride; he remembers that "after I got deferred, I wrote a letter to my interviewer thanking him again for his time and updating him as to my [deferred] status."

Connor decided to take no chances the second time around, however: "I called the admissions office and got in touch with the admissions officer in charge of my region. I made it clear to her that Harvard was my top choice and that I was still working hard during senior year to get in. She was supportive, perhaps a bit nonchalant, and said it would be fine if I send in another writing sample and a recent newspaper article. From then on I simply wrote once a month with little "updates" on what I was up to (work, academics, athletics, leadership projects)—I don't remember if she responded or not. I got accepted in the regular round."

Although his personal push seems to have been helpful, he was not sure at the time how much of an impact his effort had. As he remembers, "The admissions officer was responsive to my wishes to still go to Harvard. Overall, she was supportive enough that I wasn't intimidated, but I wouldn't say she was enthusiastic or engaged in dealing with me. I assume she did some advocating on my behalf, though."

As an aspiring track runner, Connor met the "Harvard coach before I got accepted, which helped give me an idea of the college, but it wasn't until after my acceptance that I really benefited from talking to him. By then I wasn't worried about trying to impress him, so I was able to ask critical questions that helped me make the best choice on where I wanted to go to college. My reason for meeting with the coach was initially to get my foot into the door for admissions and it was later to assess the life of a student athlete at Harvard."

At Harvard
Now that he's at Harvard, Connor has been pursuing his academics and his athletics for most of his time. He is a member of Harvard's track and cross-country team and works for HDO Training, a personal training Web site. Connor is also a member of the Spee club for men, one of the "finals clubs."

The Bottom Line
After his marathon effort to get into the school, Connor has some insights for athletes. "Applying as an athlete, I would recommend contacting the coach early on and asking for a potential trip to visit," he says. "That's the best way to both assess the school atmosphere and to meet the team and coaching staff up-front." But the visit is not only for the school. "For anyone considering athletics in college, it's essential to assess what kind of level of commitment and success you are seeking in your athletic career and how that will play into your academic goals," he continues, advising prospective applicants to look beyond the tour. "Coaches can be helpful, but often other students on the team are both more knowledgeable and more up-front."

—Scoop A. Wasserstein